FLIP the SWITCH

LIVING IN THE CHRIST LIGHT

Leader's Guide

Marcey Balcomb

Abingdon Press

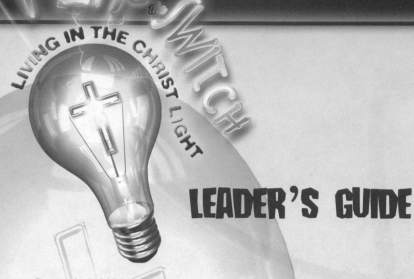

LEADER'S GUIDE

MANUFACTURED IN THE UNITED STATES OF AMERICA

Development Team
Jola Bortner
Rusty Cartee
Harriette Cross
Tim Gossett
Sharon Meads
Beth Miller
David Stewart

Editorial Team
Jennifer A. Youngman, Managing Editor
Tim Gossett, Editor
Susan Heinemann, Production Editor

Design Team
Keely J. Moore, Design Manager
Kelly Chinn, Designer

Administrative Staff
Neil M. Alexander, Publisher
Harriet Jane Olson, Vice President/Editor of Church School Resources
Bob Shell, Director of Youth Resources

CONTENTS

How to Use Faith In Motion

Leader's Guide

Information and Formation

Topic and Key Verse
This Life-to-Bible curriculum starts with important topics for junior highs and goes to God's Word.

Take-Home Learning
The goal for the session is clear.

Younger Youth and This Topic
Find out more about your youth and how they are likely to connect with this concern.

Theology and This Topic
How does Christian faith and tradition help us to understand and deal with the concern?

You and the Scripture
Our being formed as a Christian through Bible reflection and prayer is essential for our teaching.

Transformation

The Ultimate Goal: Youth will become more fully devoted disciples of Jesus Christ.

What Have You Got to Lose?

Topic: Stealing, Cheating, and Sharing

Scriptures: Ephesians 4:22-24, 28

Key Verse: "Thieves must give up stealing; rather let them labor and work honestly with their own hands, so as to have something to share with the needy" (Ephesians 4:28).

Take-Home Learning: Living in the Christ light means that we will work hard for what we have so that we can share with those in need.

Younger Youth and the Topic

The desire to steal or cheat often comes from a sense of low self-esteem. For younger youth, this desire may spring from something as simple as wanting something they can't attain easily or on their own, and the feelings that come with that realization. Some youth may not really understand why it is wrong to buy one pack of gum and just take a second one. To them, stealing an item doesn't seem like a big deal. They just want it, so they take it.

Other youth may get a sense of excitement about the idea of doing something sneaky and trying not to get caught. They may not care about the value of the item at all. This behavior is dangerous because if they succeed in stealing but don't get caught, they will likely be tempted to try it again. Many do eventually get caught and find themselves in a situation much worse than they had realized was possible.

Another common reason young people give for stealing is to get revenge or hurt someone by either damaging or taking away something they think the other person likes and values. This motive often applies to youth who steal from peers or family members.

In some cases youth may even steal to support a drug habit. Occasionally, teens will steal because they actually need something and don't know appropriate ways to get help. They may need a comb so that they can look presentable at school.

One measure that may help younger youth get a sense of whether something is right or wrong is the guilt factor. Being able to notice and identify the feelings of guilt involved in their actions, youth may be better equipped to choose to live in a way that doesn't breed those behaviors and feelings.

What Have You Got to Lose?

Theology and the Topic

Stealing or cheating causes others to lose trust in us. Our ill-chosen behaviors can easily become bad habits that damage our physical and emotional health, destroy our reputation, and challenge our faith. Like the harmful behaviors discussed in the previous sessions, stealing and cheating destroy relationships and communities.

Stealing and cheating are dishonest behaviors that we as Christians do not accept. When we hear of someone harming others, our trust and respect for that person shatters and is difficult, if not impossible, to rebuild. Most people will not invest their time and confidence in someone they do not trust. Yet God is still present, steering us toward the desire to change our ways. It is never too late to ask God for guidance and wisdom.

You and the Scripture

Read Ephesians 4:22-24, 28.

God calls us to share what we have with others. We are to be productive members of our communities. Doing so is a response to the gifts God has given us. Our lives become enriched when we care for those who are unable to work.

Sharing is a response from both the heart and from the depth of our faith. What other Scripture passages do you remember in which God's people are told to give away what they have and to share with those in need?

If giving becomes our focus, then taking from others becomes less important. Our acts of sharing show our desire to help others rather than to see how much we can gain for ourselves.

Read Ephesians 4:28 again and reflect on how this Scripture speaks to your own life. Think of some examples from your life to discuss with your youth.

Flip the Switch: Living in the Christ Light

Overview Chart
Look here for the big picture of the session. Also note the key activities, just in case time is tight.

Jump Right In!
The opening activity engages youth as they arrive.

Experience It!
Learning activities give youth a common base for making new connections.

Explore Connections
What do the Scriptures have to say? What does this mean for my life? What is a Christian to do?

Take the Challenge
The learnings are not just for Sunday!

Encounter the Holy
Ritual and mystery, prayer and commitment change hearts.

Student Journal and Reproducible Handouts

Life Focus
Topics deal with issues and concerns important to junior high youth.

Spirit Forming
The journal provides practical help and scriptural encouragement.

Group Friendly
Printed Scripture references, discussion questions, and handouts facilitate participation by individuals and small groups.

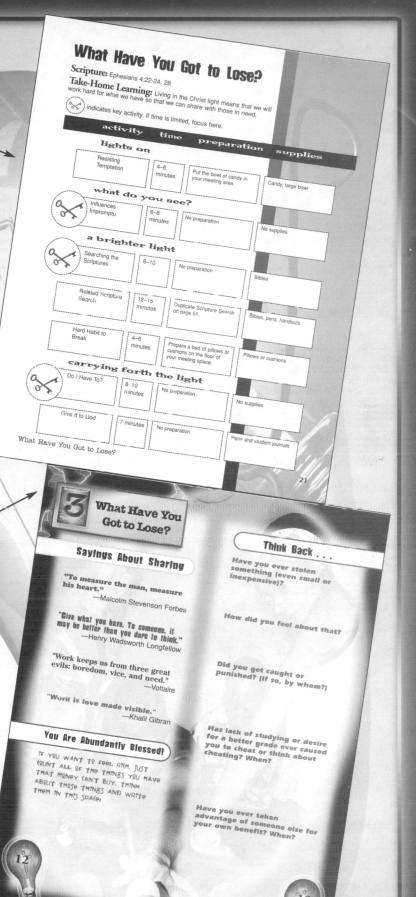

Flip the Switch?

Sometimes things happen and life changes instantly. A vow is said at an altar, and one has to check "married" rather than "single" on a tax form. A boy has a bike accident and he has to spend life in a wheelchair. A job is offered, and a family moves from one end of the country to the other. Most of these changes occur because something sudden, momentous, or unusual happens. Like the flip of a switch, life changes forever.

But most of the changes in our lives seem to happen more gradually. A successful diet or exercise plan requires time and dedication. Raising a report card from all C's to mostly A's doesn't happen in an evening. For many youth, puberty seems like a painfully long experience. And living a life of faith is truly a lifelong process.

The title of this group of lessons, FLIP THE SWITCH, implies a sudden change in some of the behaviors youth explore such as lying, swearing, and cheating. Let's be realistic: that change is probably not going to happen as a result of any particular one of your sessions. The youth you work with will likely grow in faith gradually.

So why a title like this one? The Christian tradition has always believed that sudden change is possible. Witness the transformation of Saul, or the testimonies of individuals in your church with dramatic conversion stories. At a more basic level, Christians are called to repentance by the one who started his ministry with a message to "repent, for the Kingdom of God has come near" (Matthew 4:17b). Repentance literally means to turn around and walk in the other direction. It's like flipping a switch and walking in the light.

Throughout these lessons, encourage your youth to consider a radical change of behavior. Remind them that they can head in another direction, regardless of how they have lived in the past. Encourage them when they make steps toward a new life of faith. Give them practical ideas of how to live their faith amid the messiness of their lives, and ask them to support one another as they make small and big steps of faith.

In today's world, a teenager living his or her faith is an unusual, gutsy, and radical individual. Each week as you enter your classroom and switch on the lights, let this simple action remind you that "flipping the switch" is a difficult endeavor for teens but one that can indeed shed light for all the world to see.

Truth or Lie?

Topic: Speaking the Truth Instead of Lying and Gossiping

Scriptures: Ephesians 4:22-25

Key Verse: "So then, putting away falsehood, let all of us speak the truth to our neighbors, for we are members of one another" (Ephesians 4:25).

Take-Home Learning: Living in the Christ light means honoring God by telling the truth, even when doing so is difficult.

Younger Youth and the Topic

Here's a truth that spans the generations: We tend to do and say what we have learned and practiced. We often don't think about whether it's right or wrong, loving or hurtful. We just say whatever comes out. If our minds are used to thinking the truth, we normally speak the truth. If our minds are used to making up whatever seems to fit the situation, we tell that fib. Sometimes those around us teach us to lie; other times our own lack of self-esteem or desire to be right (even when we aren't) contributes to this habit.

Most adults can sort out these concepts and realize when they have just spoken an untruth. Whether they do anything about a lie depends on how important it is to the situation. But younger youth often do not think carefully about what they say before they blurt it out. They may even embellish or exaggerate their truthful statements, blurring the line between truth and lie.

Speaking the truth in love, even when doing so is difficult, is one of the greatest gifts we can give others. Doing so strengthens relationships, deepens our feelings of belonging and acceptance, and demonstrates integrity. When we are truthful with our youth and expect them to act likewise, they usually do. In group settings, we can help them consider their responses and interactions more carefully, giving them the practice they need to think and speak the truth in their everyday lives.

Theology and the Topic

The notion of truth is mentioned throughout Scripture; as a society we often talk of how much we value truth. Yet telling the truth is difficult for many people.

In our courts today, the highest value is truth. This value is linked with biblical stories and passages in which lying is equated with evil and perversion. Proverbs 8 is an entire chapter about the gifts of wisdom, truthtelling, and insight, and the author wants nothing to do with perverted speech. In Acts 5, Ananias and Sapphira die when they tell a lie within the early Christian community. The word *truth* appears 136 times in the Bible, not counting its many derivatives and related words. Clearly, truthtelling is serious business.

Whether we tell the truth greatly affects our relationships and communities. When others discover our dishonesty, all of the things we say become suspect and the bonds of trust are broken. A reluctance to speak the truth can lead to financial coverups, adulterous affairs, and other undesirable behaviors. The most important reason to tell the truth is that we are called to be imitators of God, whom we trust above all.

You and the Scripture

Read **Ephesians 4:22-25.**

Can you think of a time in the past year when you have told a lie? Or have you just omitted some of the truth? Most of us would have to say yes, even if the lie was only a small half-truth we allowed to slide by. When you lie to someone, what do you think about afterwards? How does lying make you feel?

To get a stronger grasp on this issue, look in a concordance for additional Scriptures about truth or lying. Truthtelling is one of the most important topics you will explore with your youth.

Do you know youth who tend to "stretch" the truth or cover up their mistakes when doing so is convenient for them? Think about how you will help them explore the biblical ideas about truth and apply those ideas to their lives.

Remember, of course, that the youth learn through your example. Do the youth ever overhear you gossiping? How careful are you about disclosing information and opinions about people? Let us lead in the truth by living in the truth.

Truth or Lie?

Scripture: Ephesians 4:22-25

Take-Home Learning: Living in the Christ light means honoring God by telling the truth, even when doing so is difficult.

 indicates key activity. If time is limited, focus here.

	activity	time	preparation	supplies

lights on

	activity	time	preparation	supplies
	Put-Away Boxes	8–10 minutes	Cut the sponge into small pieces, cover the work area with newspaper, and spread the supplies out.	Small cardboard boxes, tape, sponge, acrylic or tempera paints, newspaper, cups or bowls of water, scrap paper, pencils or popsicle sticks
	Two Truths and a Lie	8–10 minutes	No preparation necessary	No supplies necessary

what do you see?

	activity	time	preparation	supplies
	Random Roles	3–5 minutes	Decide whether to read the scenarios out loud or to let a teen read them. Optional: Have the teen practice reading the scenarios.	No supplies necessary
	I've Been Lied To	6–10 minutes	Duplicate I've Been Lied To handout on page 49.	Handouts, pens or pencils

a brighter light

	activity	time	preparation	supplies
	Looking at the Scripture	9–12 minutes	No preparation necessary	Student journals
	Behind Your Back	8–11 minutes	Cut out small pieces of paper.	Small pieces of paper, index cards, pens or pencils, basket

carrying forth the light

	activity	time	preparation	supplies
	Give It to God	2–4 minutes	No preparation necessary	Student journals

Truth or Lie?

lights on

Provide one shoebox or smaller cardboard box per person, Scotch tape, small pieces of sponge, acrylic or tempera paints, newspaper, cups or bowls of water, pencils or popsicle sticks, and paper towels for cleanup.

Designate an area for drying painted boxes, and with newspaper, cover that area and the table or floor on which the youth will paint their boxes. Spread the supplies down the center of the table or floor so that they can be reached from both sides.

what do you see?

For this roleplay, you will need someone to read aloud the scenarios to the right. Either choose a youth who you think will read well out loud, or read the scenarios yourself. If you choose a youth to read, you may want to hand the Leader's Guide to him or her before the session so that the teen may practice reading.

If your group has only two youth, ask the teens to roleplay after you read each scenario out loud.

Put-Away Boxes (8–10 minutes)

When the youth arrive, invite each person to choose a box. Instruct the group to cut a slot in their boxes and to seal the lids shut with tape. Then ask the youth to each choose several colors of paint, dip a sponge into one of those colors, and dab the sponge all over the box. Tell them that blotting their sponges on the newsprint between paint applications will reduce blobs. Then instruct the group to paint the boxes using another color.

When the youth are done painting, ask them to put a few pencils or popsicle sticks under the boxes before setting them on the newspaper so that the boxes won't stick to the paper. Then ask the group members to carry their boxes to the designated area of the room where the boxes are to dry. Both acrylic and tempera paints dry quickly.

Two Truths and a Lie (8–10 minutes)

If your group is larger than fourteen, divide it into two teams. Say: "Think of three things about yourselves that you can tell the group. Two of those things should be true facts (preferably ones that most people won't already know), and one of those things should be untrue but believable. You may tell your facts in any order."

Invite each group member say his or her three statements, and ask the rest of the group to guess which statement was false. When each group member has had a turn, ask, "What's the difference between the fun of this game and a situation where you find out someone has lied to you?"

Random Roles (3–5 minutes)

Ask for two volunteers to roleplay the scenarios below, and assign those youth the roles of Characters A and B. (You will repeat this process for each scenario.) Hand your Leader's Guide to the reader and ask him or her to give the instructions below:

Scenario 1
Character A: You are skipping a class at school and are at the corner convenience store.
Character B: You are Character A's next-door neighbor's mother, who just spotted Character A in the next aisle of the store. You go to talk with him or her.
Character A, you can choose to tell the truth or a lie. You two have one minute to act out your conversation, starting now.

Scenario 2
Character A: You were invited to the birthday party of a girl you don't like. You told her you would be out of town and couldn't come to the party. Instead, you're sitting on your porch and listening to music.
Character B: You were also invited to the same party, and as you leave

your house, you see Character A sitting on her porch and listening to music. You wave and ask if she is coming to the party.

Character A, you can choose to tell the truth or a lie. You two have one minute to act out your conversation, starting now.

Scenario 3:
Character A: You are in math class, and the teacher just handed out a pop quiz. You aren't prepared, so you're trying to copy answers off Character B's paper.

Character B: You are taking your quiz and see Character A looking at it. You try to cover it up, but when Character A persists in trying to copy your paper, you get angry and say how you feel about what's going on.

Character A, you can choose to tell the truth or a lie. You two have one minute to act out your conversation, starting now.

I've Been Lied To (6–8 minutes)

Distribute copies of the I've Been Lied To handout on page 49 and pens or pencils.
Say: "Think of a time when someone you cared about lied to you. Briefly describe that situation by writing about it on the handout. A few prompts on the top of the page will help get you thinking. You may choose to use them or not. Also, think about the feelings you had when you found out you had been lied to. On the bottom part of the page, write those down, along with how you feel about it now. When you're done, fold the page and slide it through the slot in your Put-Away Box." Allow the youth some time to write.

 Looking at the Scripture (9–12 minutes)

Hand out student journals, and ask the youth to turn to "Speak the Truth!" on page 5. Ask for a volunteer to read aloud the first passage from Ephesians. Invite another youth to read the *Living Bible*'s paraphrase of Ephesians 4:25 at the bottom of the page.

Next, ask the group members to pair up with someone sitting nearby. Say: "Everyone is tempted to lie at one time or another. If the Scripture's message is 'stop lying and tell the truth,' then why is it so hard to always tell the truth? Talk with your partner about this question."

After a few minutes, tell the youth to form two circles, one inside the other, with each person facing someone in the other circle. Say: "One at a time, read aloud a quotation on page 4, or one of the Scriptures on page 5, and tell your partner what you think it means. Every thirty seconds, those in the inner circle will rotate and discuss the next quotation with their new partners. I'll let you know when each thirty-second interval is up." Begin the activity, and every thirty seconds tell those in the inner circle to rotate. End the activity by asking everyone to read aloud *The Message*'s paraphrase of Ephesians 4:25 on page 5 of the student journal.

Truth or Lie?

Provide copies of the I've Been Lied To handout on page 49 and pens or pencils.

After the session is over, put the boxes in a safe place for use in Session 5.

a brighter light

Provide student journals.

carrying forth the light

 Behind Your Back (8–11 minutes)

Hand out pieces of paper and pens or pencils to each person. Say: "A Jewish proverb says, 'What you don't see with your eyes, don't invent with your mouth.' On your slip of paper, write a comment you know was made about someone behind his or her back. We will be reading these together, but each person will read someone else's paper. You do not need to put your name on it. When you are done, fold it and drop it into this basket."

When all of the youth have dropped their papers into the basket, mix up the papers, pass the basket around, and invite everyone to draw one slip of paper, telling the students not to draw their own. Invite each person to read the comment on the slip to the rest of the group. Then ask, "What are some of the reasons people lie and gossip?"

Now hand out the index cards. Ask, "Do you ever lie to build yourself up? to break others down? to get revenge? Have you ever lied because you didn't know the whole or real truth?" Say: "On your card, write about your own habits of lying or gossiping. Your 'confession' can be general or about a specific incident, but be as truthful as you can. No one else will read what you wrote."

Give the youth a few minutes to write. Then say: "There are some things in our lives we want or need to keep to ourselves so that others don't get hurt. But we can always talk with God about these situations and ask for guidance or forgiveness. When you are done writing, put your cards in your Put-Away Boxes, so that what you have confessed on your cards is between you and God only."

Give It to God (2–4 minutes)

Say: "Let's flip the switch today on lying and gossiping. We can make a choice to act more like Christ and be honest and uplifting instead of dishonest and demeaning. Living in the Christ light means loving others so much that we want to tell them the truth and build them up."

Ask the youth take two minutes to complete pages 6 and 7 in their student journals. Then gather the youth in a circle and ask them to join hands. Read the following prayer.

"God of Truth, we know that sometimes we blame others for our own problems or shortcomings. It is hard to face our mistakes and learn from them. But we know that we can ask for your help in turning away from those habits. Remind us to practice speaking the truth with love and to care for those with whom we relate, because they deserve our honesty and respect. When friends put down other people and gossip, it's hard for us to not join in. We need your help remembering that we can choose to not be hurtful toward others. This is the way we want to be, and perhaps being kinder will even rub off on those around us. Thank you for being here for us no matter what! Amen."

Work It Out!

Topic: Acknowledging and Working Through Anger and Conflict

Scriptures: Ephesians 4:22-24, 26-27

Key Verse: "Be angry but do not sin; do not let the sun go down on your anger, and do not make room for the devil" (Ephesians 4:26-27).

Take-Home Learning: Living in the Christ light means not letting our anger get the best of us and choosing to be forgiving and compassionate.

Younger Youth and the Topic

Anger can be difficult to understand and even harder to control or handle appropriately. Younger youth still tend to respond to anger with the childish response of fighting back or becoming defensive. They may even feel the need or desire to protect themselves, reacting in a physical way.

Most often our anger is based on a need to somehow preserve our personal worth and defend our basic rights. Younger youth may easily feel rejected, dismissed, or unimportant among family or peers. They may even be told that their ideas, opinions, and feelings don't matter. Anger is often the response to that sense of disrespect or rejection.

You give youth a great gift when you help them to understand what kinds of experiences cause anger in them and explore ways they can choose to respond. Anger can be an appropriate response or a necessary step in some situations. Learning to recognize and channel that response is important to our own well-being and to others'. These lifelong skills will help youth make choices that will affect not only themselves but also those around them.

Theology and the Topic

In today's Scripture passage, at least three messages related to anger appear. First, it is OK to be angry. Sometimes anger is the most honest response. It may make us feel vulnerable as well as cautious about how to proceed. These reactions help us face certain issues and make choices that improve our lives.

Once we are angry, Paul says, we must respond in a way that does not hurt others. We should not spend our energy on finding revenge or fighting back, but on seeking God's guidance on how to handle the situation.

Work It Out!

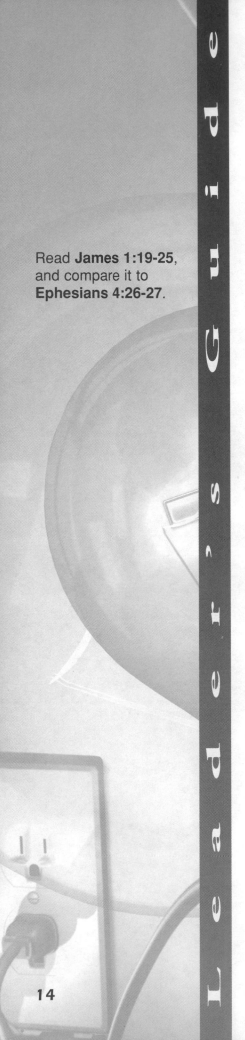

Read **James 1:19-25**, and compare it to **Ephesians 4:26-27**.

To resolve the conflict, we must find ways to move beyond anger rather than let it consume us, according to the Scripture's third message. Holding a grudge can destroy a relationship, so we must look for ways to reconcile our differences and regain trust and respect if at all possible. These obligations are especially difficult to carry out, since we often feel that our anger is justified and that someone else needs to change or give in. God can help us regain control of what's important in our lives so that we may see beyond the moment and understand whom God wants us to be.

You and the Scripture

Take a moment to think about the last time you got angry. Was your anger caused by something you did or something someone else did? In that situation, were you quick to listen and slow to anger?

When was the last time you made an effort to not let the sun go down on your anger?

Did you do everything possible to resolve the conflict rather than let it fester? Have you given up your anger rather than carrying a grudge since then?

Think about how much difficulty you have dealing with anger. Then think of a time when you felt you dealt with your anger in a way consistent with the Scripture's guidance. How did following the Scripture make a positive change in your life? You may want to tell your group about this experience.

Take a minute now to pray that God would free you from your anger. Let the love, peace, patience, joy, and kindness of our gracious God pour over you as you let go. Pray for the strength and courage to choose a loving and compassionate response when tense situations occur.

Work It Out!

Scripture: Ephesians 4:22-24, 26-27

Take-Home Learning: Living in the Christ light means not letting our anger get the best of us and choosing to be forgiving and compassionate.

 indicates key activity. If time is limited, focus here.

activity	time	preparation	supplies
lights on			
Name Those Feelings Relay	4–5 minutes	Clear a space in front of the writing surface.	Markers and markerboard; chalk and chalkboard; or a large sheet of paper, tape, easels (optional)
Stomping Out Anger	4–7 minutes	For each youth, cut a piece of yarn that is long enough to tie around his or her ankle.	Yarn and a balloon for each youth
what do you see?			
Feeling Colors	8–10 minutes	Write the color legend on page 16 a sheet of paper.	Students journals, plain paper, scissors, glue or tape, construction paper in the colors listed on page 16
a brighter light			
Anger Identification	8–10 minutes	Duplicate Anger Identification on page 54.	Handouts, pens or pencils
A Look at the Scripture	5–8 minutes	No preparation	Student journals
Resolving Conflict	4–8 minutes	No preparation	Pens, student journals, sheets of plain paper
carrying forth the light			
Refilling the Toothpaste Tube	3–4 minutes	No preparation	Travel or trial size tube of toothpaste, paper plate
Give It to God	2–4 minutes	No preparation	Student journals

lights on

Provide markers and markerboard; chalk and chalkboard; or a large sheet of paper, tape, and, if necessary, an easel for each team.

Clear a space in front of the writing surface.

Provide yarn and a balloon for each youth.

For each youth, cut a piece of yarn that is long enough to tie around his or her ankle. You may need to monitor for roughness and choose a location where the stomping noise does not disturb those in neighboring rooms.

what do you see?

Provide students journals, plain paper, scissors, glue or tape, and construction paper in the colors below.

Before the session, write the following color legend on a sheet of paper:
Blue = Sad
Green = Worried
Black = Disappointed
Pink = Lonely
Red = Angry
Yellow = Excited
Orange = Happy
White = Peaceful

 Name Those Feelings Relay (4–5 minutes)

Form two or more teams and ask each team to form a line perpendicular to the writing surface. Have the teams stand a few feet apart from one another. Give the first person in each line a marker.

Say, "When I say 'Go,' the first person in line will run to the writing surface and write a word describing a feeling. He or she will then run back and hand the marker to the next person in line, who will write another such word."

Continue the relay for two or three minutes. Keep the words on the board, easel, or wall for later use.

Stomping Out Anger (4–7 minutes)

Say: "Some of us get angry quickly and get over it quickly. Others hold onto our anger for a while and release it slowly. Either way, we're going to stomp out our anger today. Each person will get a balloon and a piece of yarn. Blow up your balloon and tie it. Tie the yarn to the balloon, then tie the other end of the yarn around your ankle so that the balloon is sticking out toward other people. Then spread out around the room."

When the youth are ready, say: "When I say 'Go,' try to stomp on other people's balloons and pop them while keeping your balloon from being popped. If your balloon pops, go to the side of the room and cheer for the others still playing. One, two, three, go!" Be sure to tell the youth that if they push or get too rough, they are automatically out.

When there's only one person left, stop the game. If his or her balloon is still intact, invite the first person who went "out" to come back in and pop it. Then ask everyone to say loudly and together, "Wow—I feel better already!"

Feeling Colors (8–10 minutes)

Invite the youth to select the colors on the legend that represent the feelings they had the last time they were angry and how they now feel about that situation. Ask the youth to cut shapes from those colors of construction paper and glue or tape them to a plain piece of paper in whatever design they choose to represent their feelings. Before the youth begin, have them look at page 8 in the student journal and select a quotation about anger that speaks to them. Tell them to write their chosen quotations on their color creations. Allow them a few minutes to complete their pictures.

When they are finished, have them form groups of three or more and show their pictures to one another, discussing how many different colors (feelings) are mixed together. Close by pointing out that while people rarely feel only one emotion at a time, strong feelings such as anger can sometimes overshadow the other feelings.

Flip the Switch: Living in the Christ Light

Anger Identification (8–10 minutes)

Hand out copies of the Anger Identification diagram on page 50 for the youth to follow as you talk. Say: "Each of us deals with anger in our own way, but three responses are common.

"Some people immediately explode with anger then either hold onto it or let it die out quickly. If you're one of these people, you tend to say things that are hurtful or that you regret because you didn't think before you lashed out. Once you have exploded with anger, you may want to just stay angry, or you might not know how to let go or get over the situation without admitting you were wrong. A more constructive alternative is to realize your response was hasty or inappropriate. Then you can move on by reconciling with or forgiving the person with whom you were angry

"A second way of responding to anger is letting it build up. By responding this way, you continue to think about what angered you. Your anger builds and builds until you feel you have to do something about it. You may continue to carry a grudge or feel the weight of your anger for a long time. Or you could decide you've spent enough time letting it build up, and reconcile or move on.

"A third way you can respond to anger is to look at the situation, acknowledge your anger, and attempt to talk through it. When you respond this way, you don't explode or store up anger. You just face it by acknowledging or naming it. You go to the source to talk through the problem and get it resolved as quickly and peacefully as possible.

"Which response best describes you? Trace your usual response to anger down the chart."

Give the youth a minute to identify their anger paths. Then have the youth get into groups of three or more, assign each group a different response to anger, and ask them to create a skit that illustrates that response. After a few minutes, invite the youth to present their skits.

 A Look at the Scripture (5–8 minutes)

Read aloud Ephesians 4:22-24, 26-27. Say: "Anger sometimes overwhelms us and causes us to act irrationally. We get so mad that we can hardly think or speak. Listen to this piece of wisdom from Proverbs 15:18: 'Those who are hot-tempered stir up strife, but those who are slow to anger calm contention.' If we think before we speak, we can respond carefully when something angers us. If we just blow up, we're likely to make the situation worse and cause continued arguments or even a violent reaction. Wanting revenge weakens us."

Ask, "Do you usually feel better about yourself when you control your anger or when you react in anger?" Invite answers with explanations and examples.

Read Ephesians 4:26-27 from *The Message*: "Go ahead and be angry. You do well to be angry—but don't use your anger as fuel for revenge.

Work It Out!

Provide copies of the Anger Identification handout on page 50 and pens or pencils.

If you have more than three groups, assign the same response to several groups. If you have fewer than nine youth, assign only one or two of the anger paths or have two-person groups.

Provide student journals.

Leader's Guide

And don't stay angry. Don't go to bed angry. Don't give the Devil that kind of foothold in your life."

Have the youth pair off to discuss the questions on page 9 in the student journal. After a few minutes, ask some volunteers how they answered the last question.

 ## Resolving Conflict (4–8 minutes)

Say: "Sometimes we get mad at ourselves, and sometimes we get mad at others. We know that getting even isn't the answer, but neither is doing nothing! Think about a situation that made you angry and that you have not taken the necessary steps to resolve. Briefly write a description of that situation in your student journal on page 11 or on a separate sheet of paper. What are some steps you can take to resolve the conflict and not carry it around anymore? Write those down and think about them each day this week."

Give the youth a few minutes to complete the activity.

Refilling the Toothpaste Tube (3–4 minutes)

Give one of the youth the toothpaste and the plate. Ask him or her to squeeze the toothpaste out of the tube and onto the plate. Have that individual hand the tube to another youth, and ask that youth to try to put the toothpaste back in the tube.

Say: "Anger and conflict are like toothpaste. When the toothpaste is out of the tube, it's pretty tough to put it back in. It's also no longer contained and under your control."

Ask: "What is the advantage of letting the toothpaste out of the tube a bit at a time, when it is needed and most useful? How does this method relate to handling anger and conflict?"

Give It to God (2–4 minutes)

Say: "As we continue to learn all that it means to live in the Christ light, let's decide that we will not let our anger get the best of us. Let's choose to be forgiving and compassionate when we start to feel anger coming on."

Invite the youth to form a circle and join hands. Ask one of the youth to read the prayer printed on page 11 of the student journal.

Provide pens and student journals; have sheets of plain paper available if students need more space to write.

carrying forth the light

Provide one travel or trial size tube of toothpaste and a paper plate.

Provide student journals.

What Have You Got to Lose?

Topic: Stealing, Cheating, and Sharing

Scriptures: Ephesians 4:22-24, 28

Key Verse: "Thieves must give up stealing; rather let them labor and work honestly with their own hands, so as to have something to share with the needy" (Ephesians 4:28).

Take-Home Learning: Living in the Christ light means that we will work hard for what we have so that we can share with those in need.

Younger Youth and the Topic

The desire to steal or cheat often comes from a sense of low self-esteem. For younger youth, this desire may spring from something as simple as wanting something they can't attain easily or on their own, and the feelings that come with that realization. Some youth may not really understand why it is wrong to buy one pack of gum and just take a second one. To them, stealing an item doesn't seem like a big deal. They just want it, so they take it.

Other youth may get a sense of excitement about the idea of doing something sneaky and trying not to get caught. They may not care about the value of the item at all. This behavior is dangerous because if they succeed in stealing but don't get caught, they will likely be tempted to try it again. Many do eventually get caught and find themselves in a situation much worse than they had realized was possible.

Another common reason young people give for stealing is to get revenge or hurt someone by either damaging or taking away something they think the other person likes and values. This motive often applies to youth who steal from peers or family members.

In some cases youth may even steal to support a drug habit. Occasionally, teens will steal because they actually need something and don't know appropriate ways to get help. They may need a comb so that they can look presentable at school.

One measure that may help younger youth get a sense of whether something is right or wrong is the guilt factor. Being able to notice and identify the feelings of guilt involved in their actions, youth may be better equipped to choose to live in a way that doesn't breed those behaviors and feelings.

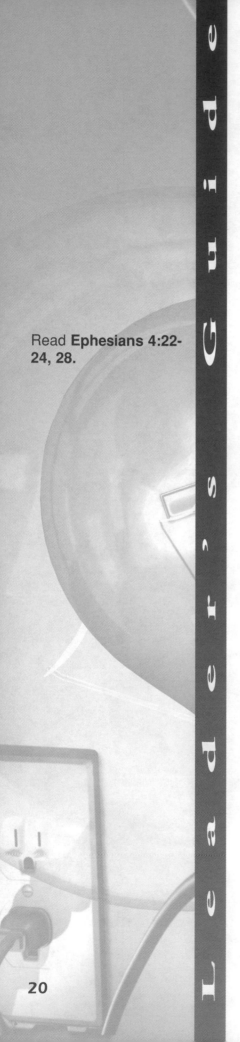

Read **Ephesians 4:22-24, 28.**

Theology and the Topic

Stealing or cheating causes others to lose trust in us. Our ill-chosen behaviors can easily become bad habits that damage our physical and emotional health, destroy our reputation, and challenge our faith. Like the harmful behaviors discussed in the previous sessions, stealing and cheating destroy relationships and communities.

Stealing and cheating are dishonest behaviors that we as Christians do not accept. When we hear of someone harming others, our trust and respect for that person shatters and is difficult, if not impossible, to rebuild. Most people will not invest their time and confidence in someone they do not trust. Yet God is still present, steering us toward the desire to change our ways. It is never too late to ask God for guidance and wisdom.

You and the Scripture

God calls us to share what we have with others. We are to be productive members of our communities. Doing so is a response to the gifts God has given us. Our lives become enriched when we care for those who are unable to work.

Sharing is a response from both the heart and from the depth of our faith. What other Scripture passages do you remember in which God's people are told to give away what they have and to share with those in need?

If giving becomes our focus, then taking from others becomes less important. Our acts of sharing show our desire to help others rather than to see how much we can gain for ourselves.

Read Ephesians 4:28 again and reflect on how this Scripture speaks to your own life. Think of some examples from your life to discuss with your youth.

What Have You Got to Lose?

Scripture: Ephesians 4:22-24, 28

Take-Home Learning: Living in the Christ light means that we will work hard for what we have so that we can share with those in need.

 indicates key activity. If time is limited, focus here.

activity	time	preparation	supplies

lights on

Resisting Temptation	4–6 minutes	Put the bowl of candy in your meeting area.	Candy, large bowl

what do you see?

Influences Impromptu	6–8 minutes	No preparation	No supplies

a brighter light

Searching the Scriptures	8–10	No preparation	Bibles
Related Scripture Search	12–15 minutes	Duplicate Scripture Search on page 51.	Bibles, pens, handouts
Hard Habit to Break	4–6 minutes	Prepare a bed of pillows or cushions on the floor of your meeting space.	Pillows or cushions

carrying forth the light

Do I Have To?	8–10 minutes	No preparation	No supplies
Give It to God	7 minutes	No preparation	Pens and student journals

lights on

Provide candy and a large bowl.

Put a large bowl of candy somewhere in the room where the youth will walk by it, but not in the area where they will gather and sit.

what do you see?

a brighter light

Provide Bibles.

Resisting Temptation (4–6 minutes)

Tell the first two youth who arrive to be "observers," who count how many times candy is taken from the bowl in the next half hour, keeping their counting to themselves. While you conduct the other activities in this session, do not specifically give permission for anyone to take the candy. (If someone asks you if he or she may have some candy, either ignore the person, or answer, "Probably.")

After you have conducted a few activities, bring the bowl to the group, and ask the observers to report their counts. Then ask:

- Did you notice the candy? If so, what did you think and feel when you saw the candy without being specifically told you could have it?

- Did the candy tempt you? Did you give in to that temptation?

- Did anyone ask permission instead of just taking it?

 Influences Impromptu (6–8 minutes)

Read the following scenario to the youth:

Patty's honors government course is her hardest class this year. Lately, her grades have dropped because the teacher grades on a curve scale. Her teacher tends to come and go from the room after giving the students a test to work on in class, and several of them share answers. Since Patty doesn't cheat, she can't fairly compete with the grades of the few who do. She's considering telling her teacher about what's been going on, but she's afraid of what the cheaters will think of her or even do to her. Will Patty let the influence of others keep her quiet? Or will she listen to the influences of her church youth group and her faith to figure out what the best solution is?

Ask for volunteers to play the roles of Patty, the teacher, and about four cheaters. Invite them roleplay a scenario in which Patty keeps quiet at the end, and another in which she decides to tell the teacher. When they are finished, ask:

- Have you ever had to make a decision like Patty's? How did you decide what to do?

- What are some positive ways you let others influence you? What about the negative ways?

- Is cheating a form of stealing? Why or why not?

 Searching the Scriptures (8–10 minutes)

Distribute the Bibles. Ask two volunteers to read aloud Ephesians 4:28 and Deuteronomy 5:19 while the others follow along.

Then say: "This verse in Deuteronomy is part of the Ten Commandments, which are set in stone. Sometimes, though, we're not exactly sure just what's considered stealing. Let's take a look at some real-life examples to see if we think they're instances of stealing." Divide the youth into teams of three or four. Read aloud the following examples, pausing after each one for a minute or two so that the youth may debate their answers; then ask each team to report its answer to the whole group, giving one reason why the team chose that answer.

1. Downloading songs—for which you paid no money—off the Internet
2. Burning a copy of one of your CDs for a friend
3. Keeping an extra dollar of change a cashier mistakenly gave you
4. Sampling a piece of individually-wrapped candy in the bulk area of the grocery store to see if you like the candy
5. Borrowing some of your sibling's clothes without asking
6. Eating food from the pantry at a house where you're babysitting (when the family didn't give you explicit permission to do so)
7. Sneaking into a second movie after the one you paid for is over

Have a few volunteers read aloud Ephesians 22-24, 28. Then say: "Our Scripture for today talks about more than just not stealing. In Ephesians, Paul tells the people to work honestly and share a portion of what they are able to gain." Ask: "When was the last time you worked for something and then shared part of it? Why, do you think, would Paul say it's important for us to share what we have with others?"

Related Scripture Search (12–15 minutes)

Hand out copies of Scripture Search on page 51 and divide the youth into groups of three or four. Say: "Spend the next seven minutes looking up the Scriptures on the sheet, and make notes in its respective bubble about what each Scripture covers."

After the youth are finished or the allotted time has passed, bring them back together to discuss what they have found. Ask each group to reflect on a different Scripture, paraphrasing its story or message. Then take a few minutes to read the verse and discuss the questions at the bottom of the handout.

Hard Habit to Break (4–6 minutes)

Ask for a volunteer to lie down on the "bed" and get comfortable. Then ask him or her to get up from the bed, and ask the other youth if they saw how hard it was to get up easily and gracefully.

Say, "Listen to this proverb: 'Bad habits are like a comfortable bed—easy to get into but hard to get out of.' " Ask: "Do any of you ever have trouble getting out of bed in the morning? What, do you think, does this proverb mean?"

If your youth group has only three or four members, form one team and ask the youth to report their answers to you.

Provide Bibles, copies of Scripture Search handout on page 51, and pens.

If your youth group has less than six members, form one team and assign each person a few of the Scriptures to look up and paraphrase.

Provide pillows or cushions.

Make a long, deep bed of pillows and cushions on the floor in your meeting space. Be sure the bed is deep enough that it will be awkward for someone to get up after lying on it.

Ask the youth to think of a few of their bad habits. Then ask them to divide into groups of two or three and discuss why it would be hard to break these habits. Allow a couple of minutes for discussion.

 **Do I Have To? (8–10 minutes)**

Ask the group the following questions:

- What are the items you own that you like the most?

- Which of these things would you be willing to give to someone who wanted them?

- What are the items you own that you need to survive?

Ask the youth to divide into groups of two or three by finding others with whom they have something in common such as a favorite brand name of clothing or another material preference. Then ask the groups the following questions, pausing after each question for discussion:

If you knew that your purchase of your favorite item would cause someone else to have an insufficient amount of food today, would you sell that item in order to provide the food that's needed? Why or why not? Would it be easier to sell that item if the money were for someone you knew or if it were someone you didn't know? Why? Would it matter why the person had no food? Why? If you wouldn't sell your favorite item, would you be willing to do some work to raise money to help provide food for that person? Why or why not?

Say, "God wants us to do honest work to obtain what we need and to share what we have with others." Ask: "Are you satisfied with how much you help provide for others in need? If not, what are two things you could do to improve your sharing habits? How could you make this change?"

Give It to God (7 minutes)

Provide pens and student journals.

Hand out the pens and student journals, and give the youth a few minutes to complete pages 12 to 15 in silence. Say: "When you think of ways you can share what you've earned with others, remember that Christ is working through you. As you live in the Christ light, you will desire to work even harder to gain more so that you can give more." Invite the group to read together the prayer printed on page 15 of the student journal. Then close by reading this prayer:

"God who meets our every need, we ask for your guidance in knowing what is right and wrong, what is helpful and hurtful, what is honest and dishonest. We realize that we don't need most of what we want. We sometimes have not earned what we ask for. Help us to give up our desires to have what is not ours and what is more than we need, and to be satisfied with what is fair and true. Keep us away from temptation and give us the desire to share what we have with others as you have taught us through your Son, Jesus Christ. Amen."

Watch Those Words

Topic: Giving Up Swearing; Building Up One Another

Scriptures: Ephesians 4:22-24, 29

Key Verse: "Let no evil talk come out of your mouths, but only what is useful for building up, as there is need, so that your words may give grace to those who hear" (Ephesians 4:29).

Take-Home Learning: Living in the Christ light means giving up words that offend or tear down and choosing to use words to respect and build up others.

Younger Youth and the Topic

Most adults have established the language they feel is appropriate to use. Younger youth, on the other hand, try on different words and expressions. Some of these words come and go with various fads, brands, movies, and activities. Many swear words, however, are learned through the generations and continue to be uttered in many ways and places.

Youth often use swear words to make an impression on others or to shock adults. Other times, they think their crude language will help them be "in" with a certain crowd. They may also believe that calling someone names will put down a person they don't like. Many older adults feel that the colorful language of youth is evidence that this generation is corrupt.

However, youth are fundamentally good people who simply out of habit use swear words and other negative terms. Young people may repeatedly hear friends and family use these words, which youth in turn speak without thinking about the words' significance. The use of sacred names in vain is also passed on in this way. As a teacher and mentor, you can help youth learn to watch their words, as well as to realize that our words can be a source of grace in the world.

Theology and the Topic

We know that God leads us toward relationships with one another. The words we use help us build or break those bonds, making us comfortable or uncomfortable, scared or calm, happy or sad.

God is present in our daily lives through the people we meet and relate to. When we are down, a positive word from a friend can pick us back up. When we are lonely, acknowledgement of our belonging can comfort us. When we feel unimportant, someone who needs us can make a world of

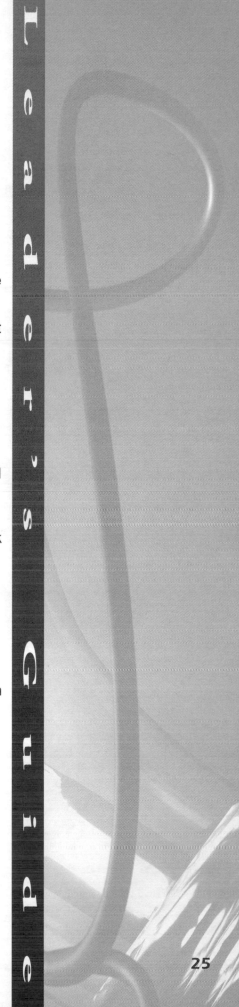

difference. These individual connections and acts of kindness are among the ways we experience the grace of God.

When we choose to give up unpleasant talk that pulls us and others down, we can replace it with words that improve how we feel about ourselves and that build up others. This week's Scripture calls us to give grace with our words. Each day, we can choose to use positive words to encourage others, or we can use words in a negative and cruel way. Think of how pleasant every day could be if we chose to lift up the positive aspects of our lives!

You and the Scripture

Read **Ephesians 4:22-24, 29.**

One dictionary's definition of the verb *to grace* is to confer dignity or honor on someone or something. In your daily life, how often do you intentionally approach a conversation or behavior with the idea of showing honor to others?

It is one thing to avoid evil talk and try to set a good example for those around us. But Ephesians reminds us to go further by thinking even more carefully about our speech, so that we may give grace with our words.

When was the last time you said something to someone specifically to build up or honor him or her?

Think about the following quotations:

- "Be honorable yourself if you wish to associate with honorable people."

—Welsh Proverb

- "What is left when honor is lost?"

—Publilius Syrus

- "A careless word may kindle strife.
  A cruel word may wreck a life.
  A timely word may level stress.
  A loving word may heal and bless."

—Anonymous

How do you give grace to others?

How can you help youth see the value of living in grace?

Flip the Switch: Living in the Christ Light

Watch Those Words

Scripture: Ephesians 4:22-24, 29

Take-Home Learning: Living in the Christ light means giving up words that offend or tear down and choosing to use words to respect and build up others.

 indicates key activity. If time is limited, focus here.

	activity	time	preparation	supplies
lights on				
	Four-Letter-Word Collage	4–6 minutes	Put the sheet of paper on a wall or room divider.	Large sheet of paper, colored markers, masking tape
	The Sack Bump	6–12 minutes	Clear a space for the youth to move around. Put objects that could easily be knocked over in a secure place.	Paper grocery sacks that are big enough to pull over someone's head
what do you see?				
	Affirmations	10–12 minutes	No preparation	Piece of individually wrapped candy for each person, index cards, pens, tape
a brighter light				
	A Word of Grace	4–6 minutes	No preparation	Bibles
	New Expressions	6–9 minutes	No preparation	Pens and student journals
	Word Search	6–8 minutes	Duplicate Word Search on page 52.	Handouts and pens or pencils, small prize (optional)
	Leather Knots	2–4 minutes	No preparation	Leather shoe lace or string for each person
carrying forth the light				
	Give It to God	2 minutes	No preparation	No supplies

Provide a large sheet of paper, colored markers, and masking tape.

Put the sheet of paper on a wall or room divider.

If your group is too large to use one big sheet, divide the youth into smaller groups and ask each group to come up with a few words that someone from the group can write on the sheet.

For each person, provide a paper grocery sack that is big enough to pull over someone's head.

Clear a space for the youth to move around. Put any objects that could easily be knocked over in a secure place.

If your group is large, you may divide it into several teams for this activity.

 Four-Letter-Word Collage (4–6 minutes)

Distribute colored markers. Invite the youth to write on the sheet of paper four-letter words that are positive or pleasing. They can write compliments, things that make them happy, and so forth. The youth may also draw pictures of what these four-letter words represent, and write words in various directions and designs.

When the youth are finished, ask them to look over the list. Say: "Sometimes we use the term *four-letter words* to refer to the words we wouldn't use in polite conversation. How are the words on the sheet of paper different from the vulgar words that sometimes come out of our mouths?"

The Sack Bump (6–12 minutes)

Distribute a paper sack to each person. Ask your group to spread out around the room. (If you know of any persons in your group who are claustrophobic, let them observe and help you monitor the group.)

Say: "Open your sack and place it over your head. When I say 'start,' you will each walk slowly around the room until you gently bump into someone. Facing him or her, with the sack still over your head, introduce yourself and tell your partner one sincere, nice thing you have observed about him or her. If you don't know your partner well, say something nice about his or her voice, or whatever you can honestly say with your limited acquaintance. Once you have exchanged compliments, mingle again until you bump into another partner. Your goal is to find every person in the room—without being able to see them—and to exchange positive expressions. You may not be able to keep track of names, but at least keep track of the number of people you talk with. I will tell you when your time is up." Address any questions the youth may have then say, "Start."

After a few minutes, have the youth take off their sacks. Ask:

- Was it easier or more difficult to say something nice to another person when you weren't looking them in the eye? Why?

- Would you rather say something nice to someone through a more impersonal method such as e-mail or a card, or by saying something nice to someone directly, person-to-person? Why?

- Would you rather receive a compliment in person or in writing? Why?

Say: "All of us love to be complimented, because it makes us feel good about ourselves and the person complimenting us. This week, pick a person you feel could use a lift, and offer him or her a sincere compliment."

Affirmations (10–12 minutes)

Distribute an index card and a pen to each person. Ask the youth to think of someone they will see soon who isn't in this group but belongs to either their congregation, homes, or schools. Then ask the youth to each write an affirmation on his or her card for that person. These affirmations should be brief, sincere notes expressing something positive about that person, and can be as simple as, "You have a great smile!"

Give the youth a few minutes to complete their affirmations, and while they are writing, pass out candy. Ask them to attach their pieces of candy to their cards with tape and set the affirmations aside for the rest of the session. At the end of the session, remind youth to take their affirmations with them, and ask them to give their affirmations to the appropriate persons as soon as possible.

 A Word of Grace (4–6 minutes)

Say: "The words we choose to use when talking with one another can help us build up or break down relationships. We often speak without realizing the affect our words may have on others and ultimately on ourselves. Our Scripture for today gives us direction in this topic. Turn to Ephesians 4:22-24 and 29, and read out loud with me." Allow time for them to find the verses, then read the Scripture in unison.

Ask, "What does it mean for our words to 'give grace to those who hear'?"

Say: "Webster's Dictionary defines the word *grace* in eight different ways. The one most closely related to today's topic is this: 'A virtue granted by God.' " Ask: "When we see someone in the hall or on the sidewalk, what could we say to that person that would give him or her a glimpse of the kind of person we are trying to be and of what God is like? What could we say to show the person that we accept him or her?"

New Expressions (6–9 minutes)

Tell the youth to think of some swear words or other negative terms they use that may offend others. Ask them to silently identify one or two they will make an effort to avoid using and indeed change in the coming week. Then ask them to look around the room (or to the list of four-letter words compiled earlier) and think of other words they could substitute for swear words.

Hand out the student journals and ask the youth to write their new expressions on page 19. Ask them to practice using the expressions during the coming week, then give them a few minutes to complete pages 16 and 17.

Provide a piece of individually wrapped candy for each person, index cards, pens, and tape.

This activity could also be done at the end of the session.

a brighter light

Provide Bibles.

Provide pens and student journals.

Note: This activity is not intended to make youth permanently abstain from using swear words; but by raising their awareness of their speech, they may be able to stop themselves before blurting out offensive words.

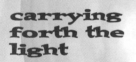

carrying forth the light

Leader's Guide

Word Search (6–8 minutes)

Distribute copies of the Word Search handout on page 52 and pens or pencils. Let them have fun finding positive words. If you wish, you may give a small prize to whoever comes up with the most words during the allotted time.

Leather Knots (2–4 minutes)

Give each group member a leather shoe lace or string. Ask the youth to tie five knots anywhere on the lace. Say: "Here's a visual way to keep track of how you are doing with your use of put-downs. Carry this shoe lace with you for the next two weeks. You might tie it to your key chain or make a necklace out of it. Each time you say a put-down or anything that is not nice to another person, tie a knot in the lace. Each time you say something to build up another person, you may untie a knot. I'll remind you to bring your shoe lace with you to class two weeks from now so that we can talk about how everyone has done."

Be sure to make a note to yourself to call the youth the day before Session 6 to remind them about bringing the shoe lace.

Give It to God (2 minutes)

Say, "When you hear yourself speaking words that may hurt or offend others, imagine that you have a light switch in your hand that you can just flip so that your language honors God."

Invite the youth to form a circle and join hands. Ask one of the youth to read aloud the prayer printed on page 19 of the student book. Close your prayer time by reading this prayer:

"God of Grace, we know that you give us love and honor, not because we deserve it or earn it, but because they are free gifts from you. We believe that our responsibility is to use your gifts to build up others and to help them become the best they can be. Please remind us of this responsibility when our language becomes a barrier rather than a bridge, when our hearts become closed and hard rather than open and caring. Help us to hear the hurtful words we are about to say and to replace them with words of grace and hope. We pray in the name of your Son, Jesus Christ. Amen."

Lighten the Load

Topic: Hate and Forgiveness

Scriptures: Ephesians 4:22-24, 31-32

Key Verse: "Put away from you all bitterness and wrath and anger and wrangling and slander, together with all malice, and be kind to one another, tenderhearted, forgiving one another, as God in Christ has forgiven you" (Ephesians 4:31-32).

Take-Home Learning: Living in the Christ light means that hating people is not an option. We are called to love, forgiveness, and kindness.

Younger Youth and the Topic

Younger youth easily get angry at someone—even a good friend—and exclaim they'll never talk to that person again. Some youth even decide on a daily basis to whom they will be nice. They may choose others to ignore or to be mean to.

Younger youth may behave this way partly because they have difficulty seeing the long-term damage their negative actions can do to their relationships. For many younger youth, their primary concern is themselves. If someone has done or said something to hurt them, a long time may pass before they will give that person a chance to reconcile, if ever.

When younger youth stay angry, they may watch for opportunities for revenge, a habit that gets in the way of forgiveness. These youth may also quickly claim someone else as their new best friend and devote their loyalty to the new friend or group.

Younger youth need to learn about forgiveness and the joy that can come from being kind and helpful to others. This type of behavior should be normative and encouraged every week in your meeting place.

Theology and the Topic

The Ephesians passage reminds us how we are to live the new life. It spells out what we must give up and in which direction we must go instead. The focus is as much about adopting new ways of living as it is about shedding the old ways. But the only way to truly move on is to get rid of our heavy loads.

These loads may include bitterness, grudges, painful memories, and even malice and hate. These weigh us down, making our days seem drawn out,

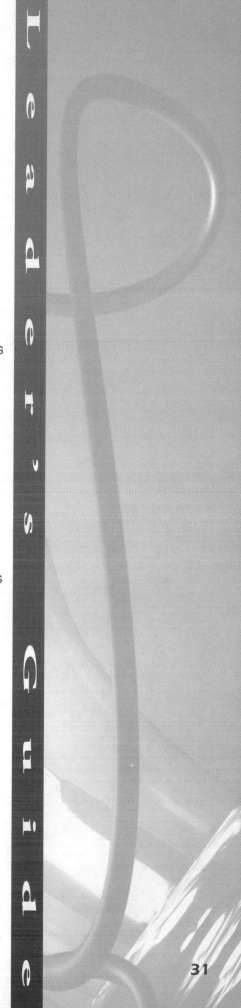

Lighten the Load

Read **Ephesians 4:22-24, 31.**

and preventing us from experiencing what God intends for us: wholeness in all our relationships.

The Scripture commands us to overcome our heavy baggage by finding ways to forgive in our daily lives. God in Christ has forgiven us, and we must learn to do the same for one another.

You and the Scripture

To prepare yourself for this session, reflect on these questions by listening to your heart and answer them honestly.

- Do you remember a time when you were hurt by someone? Describe it.

- Do you remember a time when you hurt someone? Describe it.

- What relationship in your life is painful or needs healing?

- How often do you think of these issues?

- Do they sometimes keep you from having a positive attitude or from moving forward? How so?

- When will you give in and lighten your load?

God is always ready to help you with your load. Take a minute now to ask.

Lighten the Load

Scripture: Ephesians 4:22-24, 31

Take-Home Learning: Living in the Christ light means that hating people is not an option. We are called to love, forgiveness, and kindness.

 indicates key activity. If time is limited, focus here.

	activity	time	preparation	supplies
lights on				
	Words That Hurt	6–8 minutes	Place the "Put Away Boxes" from Session 1 in a space where the youth can access them.	Index cards, pens or pencils, "Put Away" Boxes from Session 1
	Lighten Up	12–15 minutes	If necessary, reserve a large room. With masking tape mark two lines at least fifteen feet apart, leaving plenty of space behind both lines.	Balloons, one egg-size rock, one permanent marker per team, masking tape
what do you see?				
	What's Your Outlook?	3–6 minutes	No preparation	Bibles, index cards, pens or pencils
	A Lighter Load	4–7 minutes	No preparation	Pens, student journals, CD or cassette tape of soft music and CD or cassette player (optional)
a brighter light				
	Healing the Wounds	8–10 minutes	Divide bandage strips into sets of three. For each set write GOD WILL on the first strip, HEAL on the second, and YOUR WOUNDS on the third.	Pencils, pens, red construction paper, scissors, small adhesive bandage strips
	Forgiving Again and Again	5–10 minutes	No preparation	Popsicle sticks, thin-point markers
carrying forth the light				
	Give It to God	2 minutes	Duplicate My Prayer of Forgiveness handout on page 53.	Pens or pencils, handouts

Provide index cards, pens or pencils, and the "Put Away" Boxes from Session 1.

Prior to the session, place the "Put Away" Boxes in a space where the youth can access them.

This activity may bring back painful memories for some youth. Be sensitive to those youth. You may also want to monitor for obscene language when the group discusses their words.

Provide balloons, one egg-size rock and one permanent marker per team, and masking tape.

Prior to the session, you may want to reserve a large room for this activity.

Clear a large space in the room. With masking tape mark a Line 1 and a Line 2 at least fifteen feet apart, leaving space at one side of Line 1 for the youth to line up, and space at the opposite side of Line 2 for lots of filled balloons.

Words That Hurt (6–8 minutes)

Hand out a pen and an index card to each person. Say: "One of the ways we express our bitterness or hatred is by using words that hurt others. Think of some of the words you have used to express yourself when feeling angry or bitter, and write them on your card."

After two minutes, ask the youth who are comfortable with telling the group some of these words to do so.

Then say, "Think of some words that describe your feelings when you have been hurt, and write those words on the other side of your card."

After two minutes, ask the youth who are comfortable with telling the group some of these words to do so. Finally, ask the youth to put the cards in their "Put Away" Boxes.

 ## Lighten Up (12–15 minutes)

Divide the youth into two or more teams for a relay. Ask each person to blow up a balloon, tie it closed, and place it behind Line 2. Then ask the youth to line up as teams behind Line 1. Give the first person in each line a marker.

Say: "The balloons represent good things we can do or say to make up for the hurtful things we have done. In this relay, you will run, one at a time, to write on a balloon a word or phrase of kindness or forgiveness. Then bring the balloon back to the line you're now behind and put it in your team's pile. When everyone on your team has brought a balloon, the whole team should sit down." Address any questions the youth may have, then say, "Ready, set, go!"

Let the youth play until every team has finished. When all of the teams are sitting, ask the youth to form a circle with their team members, placing all of their balloons in the middle. Give each team one rock. Ask them to pass the rock around and feel how heavy it weighs. Then ask, "How many balloons, do you think, would it take to add up to the weight of the rock?"

Say: "For each rock we throw, or each hurtful thing we say or do, it takes many more kind and helpful things to bring healing or forgiveness. Think about this fact the next time you are tempted to say something rude or unkind to someone."

What's Your Outlook? (3–6 minutes)

Hand out Bibles, and have the group read Ephesians 4:22-24, 31-32 together in unison.

Hand out two index cards and a pen or pencil to each person. Say: "Think of the people you see fairly often at school, at home, or at church. Do you know any people who usually seem sad, grumpy, angry, or even mean? Write their names or initials on one of your cards. If you don't know someone's name or initials, invent a name. You won't have to show these cards to anyone else."

Allow the youth time to think and write. Then say: "Take a moment to imagine how those people feel each day and how their negative outlook or actions must affect them. On the back of the same card, write a sentence or several words describing how you imagine they feel."

Give the youth time to think and write. Ask, "Can you identify other people who usually seem content or have a positive attitude about life?" Say: "On your second card, write their names or initials. On the back of the same card, write how you imagine they feel each day."

Allow the youth time to think and write, then invite them to join you in prayer. Pray: "God of understanding and forgiveness, we ask that you would be close to the people we named on our first cards and help them to find ways to move past their negative feelings and see the good in themselves and others. Let them feel your presence and comfort when life seems difficult. We also pray for those around us who have chosen to see and live life in a positive way. We thank you for their joy and how we feel when we are around them. Lord, we ask you to open our hearts to your love and forgiveness and to lead us in your way. Amen."

A Lighter Load (4–7 minutes)

Hand out the pens and student journals. Have the youth read page 20 and then complete "Sometimes It's Hard to Forgive" on page 21 and "Walking the Forgiveness Road" on pages 22 and 23. You may wish to play some soft music in the background to help the youth remain quiet and focused.

Healing the Wounds (8–10 minutes)

Pass out the supplies. Invite each youth to draw a large heart on his or her sheet of construction paper with a pencil and cut it out.

Then say, "Write on your heart three words that hurt you or others." Give the youth a minute to think and write.

Give each person a set of three adhesive bandage strips. Invite the youth to place a bandage over each wound on their hearts in a way that

what do you see?

Provide Bibles, index cards, and pens or pencils.

Provide pens and student journals. Optional: a CD or cassette tape of soft music and a CD or cassette player.

a brighter light

Provide pencils, pens, red construction paper, scissors, and small adhesive bandage strips.

Divide the bandage strips into sets of three. For each set write *GOD WILL* on the first bandage, *HEAL* on the second, and *YOUR WOUNDS* on the third.

makes the phrase GOD WILL HEAL YOUR WOUNDS readable. Say: "We know that, as surely as we have placed bandages on the wounds of our hearts, God is already at work healing us and helping us release these burdens."

 Forgiving Again and Again (5–10 minutes)

Provide popsicle sticks and thin-point markers.

Give each youth ten popsicle sticks and a marker. Then say: "Think about your interactions with others that have made you happy. When was the last time you said or did something nice for someone that made you feel good? When was someone you didn't know very well nice to you? For every unkind act or word we experience or hear, there are many kind and friendly ones. On each stick, write an act or word of kindness that you like to do or see others do."

Allow the youth three minutes to write. Then invite them to form a circle around the table or on the floor. (If your group is large, ask the youth to form two circles.) Tell them that they are going to build a symbol of kindness that represents their group. Ask the group members to take turns putting one stick at a time on the table or floor, building a symbol in which every stick is touching another stick. Tell them that the symbol can be any shape, two dimensional or three dimensional.

When the symbol is complete, say: "If we were to intentionally practice each of these kindnesses this week, both our lives and the lives of others would change for the better. Let's see what a positive difference we can make!"

carrying forth the light

Provide pens or pencils and copies of My Prayer of Forgiveness handout on page 53.

Note:
As the session ends, remind the youth about their leather knots from Session 4. Ask them if they have tied or untied any knots since that session.

Give It to God (2 minutes)

Distribute copies of My Prayer of Forgiveness handout on page 53 and pens or pencils. Ask the youth to find a place in the room where they can complete this exercise in solitude. Tell them they will be writing a closing prayer, using the worksheet provided.

Give them a short time to work. Say: "This week as we leave, let's decide that we will choose love and forgiveness over hate. Remind yourself every day that to have true joy you cannot have hate in your heart." Then ask for volunteers to read their prayers as the closing of the session.

Flip the Switch: Living in the Christ Light

On the Outs

Topic: Choosing Words of Thanksgiving Over Obscene, Vulgar, and Empty Talk

Scriptures: Ephesians 4:22-24; 5:1-2, 4, 6-7

Key Verse: "Entirely out of place is obscene, silly, and vulgar talk; but instead, let there be thanksgiving. . . . Let no one deceive you with empty words, for because of these things the wrath of God comes on those who are disobedient" (Ephesians 5:4, 6).

Take-Home Learning: Living in the Christ light means expressing the joy of Christ and giving thanks to God instead of joining in talk that is trivial or offensive.

Younger Youth and the Topic

"Trying on" borderline talk and behaviors intrigues middle schoolers, who often stretch rules and push their behavior beyond the acceptable boundaries. They are experimenting partly to know more clearly where their boundaries are. Although youth complain about them, boundaries often comfort young people by giving them a way to choose right over wrong, especially when other youth encourage them to do something risky, deceptive, or disobedient.

Youth this age focus on socializing and trying out new ways to relate, look, or express themselves as unique individuals. When given an opportunity to talk about their moral choices, however, they can understand that their behavior may help them fit into one group, but harm their relationships with family and other friends. Belonging is important to their self-esteem, and the church offers them opportunities to fit in without trying on harmful behaviors. The church might be the only place where a teen feels like he or she truly belongs.

A hard but important lesson for youth to learn is that obscene or offensive language and actions most often leaves them on the outside of the social circle. If teens spend some of their energy doing and expressing positive things, they will feel more connected to their social environment and feel better about themselves. Their positive actions can even be contagious!

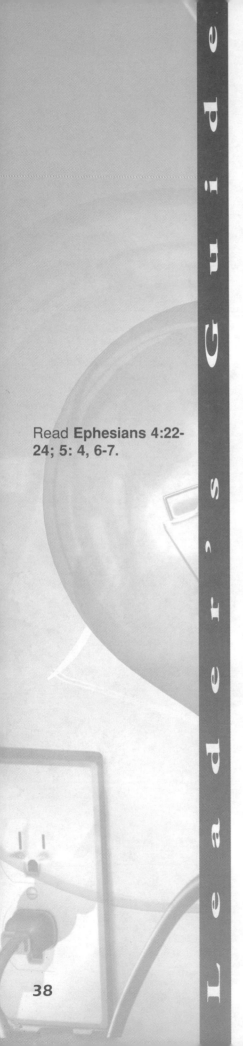

Theology and the Topic

The Scripture for this session calls us to be imitators of God, to live in love as Christ loved us. Our lives can be filled with joy and thanksgiving when we are faithful to the lessons Jesus taught. This promise doesn't mean that all of life will be a "bowl of cherries," but it does mean that we get to determine, to a large degree, how we will live our lives. We can choose to focus on God's goodness, thanking the Lord for all we have and continue to receive.

Each of us is responsible for our words and actions and the messages they give to those who hear or observe them. Actions flow from character. Living in the Christ light means living with integrity and being the light of a darkened world.

Nelson Mandela once said, "We must use time wisely and forever realize that the time is always ripe to do right." May there be thanksgiving in our everyday lives!

You and the Scripture

Proverbs 10:9 says, "Whoever walks in integrity walks securely, but whoever follows perverse ways will be found out."

Can you think of a time when someone in a group you were with made vulgar comments or told coarse jokes and everyone laughed as though the comments or jokes were OK? Did you go along with the laughter? Were you uncomfortable with the laughter? Were you brave enough to let them know you were uncomfortable or felt the comments were inappropriate? If many adults have difficulty speaking up in these situations, we should not be surprised that younger youth often find it impossible to do so.

The best way to influence the youth with whom we work is to live as examples of what the Scriptures tell us about the nature and image of God. We have a responsibility to care about what people say to one another and how they treat one another.

Read Ephesians 5:4, 6-7 again. What is one thing you feel you need to work on that relates to these particular passages? Why?

Consider discussing your own struggles with the youth during your conversations on this topic. They'll benefit from your honesty.

Read **Ephesians 4:22-24; 5: 4, 6-7.**

Flip the Switch: Living in the Christ Light

On the Outs

Scripture: Ephesians 4:22-24; 5:1-2, 4, 6-7

Take-Home Learning: Living in the Christ light means expressing the joy of Christ and giving thanks to God instead of joining in talk that is trivial or offensive.

 indicates key activity. If time is limited, focus here.

activity	time	preparation	supplies
lights on			
Remember the Joke About . . . ?	5–7 minutes	On a large writing surface, write *NO JOKE*.	Writing surface, marker or chalk, paper, pens, and at least one small adhesive paper square per person
May I Go With You?	4–6 minutes	Duplicate May I Go With You? handout on page 54 and write *GOD* on each nametag.	Handouts and one nametag for each group of six
what do you see?			
Sticky Situations	8–13 minutes	On separate sticky notes, write the phrases listed on page 40.	Bible
a brighter light			
Let There Be Thanksgiving!	8–10 minutes	Reproduce the letters and blank spaces from the handout onto the large writing surface.	Handouts; pencils; chalk and chalkboard, markers and markerboard, or markers and a large sheet of paper
What God Mostly Does Is Love You!	6–8 minutes	Cut out a long, narrow paper heart for each group member as a bookmark.	Paper, pens or pencils, scissors
Imitations	5–7 minutes	No preparation	No supplies
carrying forth the light			
Give It to God	2 minutes	No preparation	No supplies

Provide a large writing surface, chalk or a marker, pens, and at least one small adhesive paper square per person.

Prior to the session, write NO JOKE on the large writing surface.

Provide copies of May I Go With You? handout on page 54 and one nametag per group.

Write GOD on each nametag.

If your youth group is smaller than six, ask for a volunteer to be "God," and have the other youth alternate in reading the statements.

what do you see?

Provide a Bible.

Before the session, write the following phrases on separate sticky notes: Stealing a candy bar; Lying to your parents; Cheating on a test; Betraying a friend's confidence; Skipping school; Placing blame on someone innocent; Damaging someone else's property; Making fun of a teacher; Starting a rumor; Denying involvement in something wrong that you took part in.

Remember the Joke About...? (5–7 minutes)

Distribute the paper squares and pens to the group. Say: "People often use jokes to make fun of individuals or groups of people. The punch line to the joke usually implies that someone or some group is stupid, gullible, or has some other negative trait. People laugh when they hear the jokes for one of two reasons: either they believe the stereotype of the individual or group being made fun of, or they feel that they are expected to laugh—they laugh because they don't want to be left out.

"Jesus Christ taught that people who are different from us should be loved, not made fun of. To emphasis that these 'jokes' are not really jokes, we have posted a NO JOKE space. On each of your paper squares, write a word or short phrase that describes a group of people generalized in the jokes you hear. These persons might be ethnic groups, genders, people with certain physical traits, and so on. When you've finished writing, tape your squares in the space labeled *NO JOKE*. Then open your student journals to page 26 and answer the first three questions."

Ask for volunteers to tell the group what they wrote in their journals, and engage in any other conversation the youths' ideas may spark.

May I Go With You? (4–6 minutes)

Divide the youth into groups of six. Ask for a volunteer in each group to be "God" for this activity. Say, "The rest of you are Readers and should form a circle around your group's 'God' and number off from one to five."

Then distribute a copy of the May I Go With You? handout to the number one Reader in each group. Say: "One at a time, the Readers will step into the circle, stand in front of 'God,' and read the statements corresponding to their numbers. 'God' will turn to that person and respond with the phrase *May I go with you?*"

After all of the statements have been read, say, "Discuss with your group how your actions and feelings would change if you remembered that God goes with you wherever you go and whatever you do."

Sticky Situations (8–13 minutes)

Hand a Bible to a youth and invite him or her to read aloud Ephesians 5:1-2, 4, 6-7. Then pass around the sticky notes.

Ask the youth to line up in a row, facing you. (Multiple lines are fine in a large group.) Say: "Put your sticky note on the back of the person in front of you. The first person in line should put his or her note on the last person in line." After the youth have assigned the notes, ask them to pair off, beginning at the front of line. (If there is an odd number of youth, allow one group of three.) Then ask them to read aloud the sticky note on their partners' backs. Say: "Imagine that someone has talked you into doing this particular action. How do you feel about having behaved that way? Act out for your partner how you would feel."

After the youth have had time to roleplay, gather the groups and say: "Think of a time when you were talked into doing something you knew was wrong. Now think about who it was who talked you into doing it. Perhaps the person was a friend, sibling, classmate, or neighbor. Can you tell us why you went along with that person?" Let any youth who wish to answer do so.

Invite another youth to read Proverbs 10:9 to the group. Ask, "What does this proverb remind us about our words and actions?"

Say: "When we allow friends who make poor choices to talk us into doing something wrong, not only will others find out and possibly lead to unpleasant consequences—God will also know what we have done. We can choose to live in a way that exposes our desire to sin, or we can live in a way that reflects the light of Christ. The more we 'put on' good character, the more others see Christ in us. Likewise, the more we use offensive language, harm others, and make them feel uncomfortable, the worse we feel about ourselves, the worse our reputation becomes, and the less integrity we demonstrate."

Hand out the student journals and ask the youth to complete pages 24–27.

 ## Let There Be Thanksgiving! (8–10 minutes)

Hand out pencils and copies of Let There Be Thanksgiving! handout on page 54. Say: "Down the left side of the page is the word *Thanksgiving*. Beside each letter of this word there is space to write a word that starts with that letter. Think of words that are pleasing, positive, Christlike, or in today's Scripture, and fill in the blanks."

When most of the youth are done, invite them to tell the group what they wrote. As they do so, compile a larger list of their words for each letter on the chalkboard, markerboard, or large sheet of paper.

Ask, "Which of these words would describe what we would do or be if we were 'imitators of God,' as the Scripture instructs?"

Divide the youth into groups of two or three and ask the groups to discuss the following questions: Which of these qualities in the list do you exhibit the best? Which of these qualities do you need to exhibit more often?

What God Mostly Does Is Love You! (6–8 minutes)

Distribute a paper heart and pen or pencil to each person. Say: "We know that God wants us to live as Christ loved us, but we also know we don't always live up to that expectation. God helps us see our

On the Outs

a brighter light

Provide copies of Let There Be Thanksgiving! handout on page 54; pencils; chalk and chalk board, markers and markerboard, or markers and a large sheet of paper.

Reproduce the letters and blank spaces from the handout onto the large writing surface.

Provide paper, pens or pencils, and scissors.

Prior to the session, cut out a long, narrow paper heart for each group member as a bookmark.

wrongdoings and change our ways. But what God mostly does is love us! On your paper heart, write or draw pictures of some ways we know God shows us love."

When the youth are done, say, "Take your heart home and put it in a school book or other book as a reminder God's love."

Imitations (5–7 minutes)

Ask everyone to find a partner and stand facing him or her. Be sure the partners are a few feet apart.

Say: "The person with the smaller feet will be the leader, and the other person will be the imitator. Leaders, put your hands up, palms facing the other person. Imitators, put your hands up to 'mirror' the leader's actions. The leaders can now move their hands around in any direction or pattern, and the imitators should match the movements to mirror the leaders' hands. The point is to be able to move together perfectly and smoothly. See how well you can work together."

Give the first leaders one minute to be mirrored, then ask the youth to reverse roles. After another minute, have the youth come back together. Ask:

- Leaders, how did it feel to lead hoping your partner could follow?

- Imitators, was it hard or easy to follow your leader? Why? How was following your leader like following God?

- What can you do every day to follow and imitate God?

Give It to God (2 minutes)

Invite the youth to form a circle and join hands. Say: "Living in the light of Christ means showing love to everyone and standing up for outcasts. When you find yourself in a situation where someone is making fun of a person or a group of people, think to yourself: How can I shine the light of Christ into this situation? When you're involved in something that is not an imitation of God, think about how the presence of God in you can change or improve the situation. Let's pray.

"God, we want to belong to you and live in love as Christ loved us, but doing so isn't easy. We try to imitate you, but we aren't always sure what you want us to do. Help us to see your way more clearly. Remind us of it when our words or actions cause us to be out of place, and guide us back to the ways of love and kindness. Help us to replace our 'out-of-place' talk with words of thanksgiving and praise for all you are and do for us. We want to live in the light of your love and reflect your goodness in our actions. Help us to see all of the things in our lives that are cause for thanksgiving and joy. We know that in you we will always find acceptance and a place to be at home. Amen."

If you have an odd number of youth in your group, either do the activity with one of them, or give the group an extra minute and allow someone to lead two youth.

carrying forth the light

Note:
As the session ends, remind the youth about their leather knots from Session 4. Ask them if they have tied or untied any knots since that session.

Flip the Switch: Living in the Christ Light

Don't Mention It

Topic: Sex, Greed, Materialism, and Drugs

Scriptures: Ephesians 5:3, 5

Key Verse: "But fornication and impurity of any kind, or greed, must not even be mentioned among you, as is proper among saints" (Ephesians 5:3).

Take-Home Learning: Living in the Christ light means not giving in to sexual temptations, greediness, and the temptation to harm the body with drugs and alcohol.

Younger Youth and the Topic

We would like to think that the topics listed above do not concern younger youth and that our youth have not had any of these experiences. Their age range, however, is when much of the experimenting in these areas begins and takes hold. And, as with many bad habits, once youth begin engaging in these behaviors, they often feel resigned, thinking that since the mistakes are already made, they might as well go ahead and continue the habit.

This is a perfect time to talk with youth about starting over. This change is especially important for sexual activity. If they can no longer claim virginity, they may feel as though they are forever marked. Yet they can still choose to reclaim abstinence.

It is also not too late for youth to evaluate which persons have a negative influence on them. They should take the time to consider who encourages them to choose destructive behaviors and even challenges them to continue those actions.

Prepare yourself for conversations that may reveal serious problems and inappropriate, if not criminal, behaviors such as abuse and incest. If your ears are open, you might hear a story about a parent providing the booze for a youth's party, or leaving the youth home alone with plenty of opportunity for sexual activity or drug use. Remember that you may be legally required to report suspicions and comments that reveal these behaviors, and the youth need to know that you might take such action if they choose to share certain information with you.

They are also immersed in materialism and greed. Extremely conscious of fashions and trends, younger youth believe that having the right items or brands will put them in the right crowd. Help them hear the message that they are called to choose a life that does not worship things.

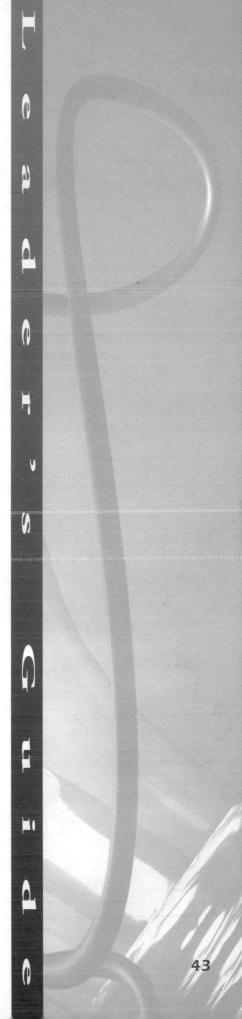

Theology and the Topic

Why should we rid ourselves of lustful thoughts, harmful substances, and wasteful habits? For Paul, the issue is one of purity. As members of the community in Christ, we are to imitate God, who is pure and holy, and in whose image we were created. We are also to imitate Christ's love, which is not the "love" in obscene websites or the "love" we have for a favorite brand of jeans.

Some youth leaders feel uncomfortable discussing topics like these because they remember their previous behaviors with regret or shame. Others still struggle to fully put on their new selves, and thus feel like hypocrites when they address these issues with youth. The truth is that we all make poor decisions sometimes, and no one is immune from the pressures of society, family, and friends. Yet God's grace is continually active, convicting us of sin and sanctifying our lives. We can teach knowing that no previous action is unforgivable and no present habit is unbreakable.

You and the Scripture

As you read carefully the entire section of Ephesians that we have been studying, think about how each of the instructions is a way of putting away the former ways of life and putting on a new self. Ask yourself: Why are these new ways of life critical for the faith community? Why must the members of the body of Christ look, sound, and act differently from the rest of the world?

Spend some time thinking about how you have dealt and now deal with these topics, as well as how you are handling the stumbling blocks or damaged relationships that are results of the behaviors Paul condemns. If the problems are resolved, great. If not, make a commitment to yourself to work on those areas, at least one at a time. A review that helps you put your life in perspective will prepare you for talking with youth about the Ephesians passage without your own behaviors or desires getting in the way of an honest conversation.

Finish your review and reflection time with prayer, knowing that forgiveness is always available from God when we ask.

Don't Mention It

Scripture: Ephesians 5:3, 5

Take-Home Learning: Living in the Christ light means not giving in to sexual temptations, greediness, and the temptation to harm the body with drugs and alcohol.

 indicates key activity. If time is limited, focus here.

activity	time	preparation	supplies
lights on			
Enough of the Right Stuff	8–10 minutes	Cut out a giant paper doll and tape it to a wall or door.	Markers, a large roll of paper, scissors, and masking tape
Surrounded by Sex	9–14 minutes	Gather issues of popular magazines (including teen magazines).	Popular magazines, paper, and pens or pencils
what do you see?			
The Great Escape	10–12 minutes	No preparation	Markers and posterboard or large sheets of paper, markerboard or chalkboard and chalk (optional)
a brighter light			
Here and Now	10–12 minutes	Duplicate Considering My Choices handout on page 55.	Handouts, pens or pencils, a student journal
One Message, Three Versions	4–6 minutes	No preparation	Student journals
carrying forth the light			
It Isn't Too Late!	5 minutes	No preparation	Student journals
Give It to God	2 minutes	No preparation	No supplies

Don't Mention It

Provide markers, a large roll of paper, scissors, and masking tape.

Before the session, you may cut out a giant paper doll, or you may have the first youth who arrive trace and make a paper cutout of the shape of one of their bodies. Hang the paper cutout on a wall or door with masking tape.

Provide popular magazines (including teen magazines), paper, and pens or pencils.

If your group is small, divide it into two teams and assign each team two of the group activities.

Enough of the Right Stuff (8–10 minutes)

Say: "Think of the popular name-brand clothes you have. When you've thought of the brand names, come up to the paper cutout and write those names on the body parts that correspond to those names. For example, you might write a popular brand of shoes on the feet of this paper person."

Hand out the markers and give the youth a minute to complete this task. Then ask:

- What makes these brands so popular?

- Is it important to you to have the "right" brand or style to match others at school? Why or why not?

- Do these brands cost more, the same, or less than similar clothes?

- Do your friends ever make comments about the clothes that you or others wear? How do those comments make you feel?

- What are the downsides of trying to have all of the popular brands and follow all of the latest trends?

- In what way does greed play a role in what young people buy?

Divide the youth into groups of three, and invite them to discuss these questions:

- Do you have more things than you actually need or even want?

- What do you have that you could give away to someone who needs it more than you do?

Surrounded by Sex (9–14 minutes)

Divide the youth into four groups. Say: "Each group will be thinking about how sex is more a part of our lives than we realize. Group One: I'd like you to make a list of all the places and ways you are exposed to sexual behavior, jokes, images, music, and dialogue. Group Two: I'd like you to look through these magazines and make a list of all of the ads that use sex appeal to sell something. Group Three: I'd like you to make a list of all of the songs you can think of that have to do with sex. Group Four: I'd like you to make a list of all of the movies and television shows you can think of that demonstrate casual sex as the norm. Each group will have five minutes to make their lists."

Hand out the paper, pens or pencils, and magazines. After five minutes, invite the youth to read their lists to the entire group. Then ask:

- Do you think it's fair to say that you're surrounded by sex? Why or why not?

- Why, do you think, is so much emphasis placed on sex and sexiness today, even among teenagers?

- In what ways does focusing on sex treat people as objects rather than children of God?

Flip the Switch: Living in the Christ Light

Leader's Guide

Carrying forth the light

Provide student journals.

Provide student journals.

✂ One Message, Three Versions (4–6 minutes)

Hand out student journals, ask the group to turn to page 28, and invite three youth to read aloud one of the three versions of the Ephesians passage. Ask:

- According to this Scripture, to what things are we to say no? Why? What are the consequences of indulging in them?
- Why did Paul want the people of Ephesus to avoid even mentioning sexual immorality, greed, or idolatry?
- How would your life be different if you took this passage seriously?
- How difficult would it be to follow Paul's instruction? Why?

It Isn't Too Late! (5 minutes)

Say: "No matter what we have done in the past, God is always ready to forgive us and give us another chance if we sincerely want to change our behavior. It isn't too late to get a fresh start and make better choices. Some of our past actions may have long-term consequences if we hurt ourselves or others, but our souls can be made new if we ask. On page 30 of your journal, write three things you would like God to forgive you for or help you change. No one else will see what you write. When you are finished, take a minute to think or pray about what you've written."

Say: "As we grow closer to Christ, the desire for lots of stuff lessens. We also become more secure with ourselves and do not need to prove anything by pushing sexual boundaries. Christ calls us to depend on him and show self-control with our bodies and our resources. When you feel tempted in any way, turn to Christ, who knows what temptation feels like and can get you through it."

Give It to God (2 minutes)

Ask a youth to read the question and paragraph in "Wash It Away" on page 31 in the student journal. Spend a moment in quiet reflection and close with the following prayer:

"God of all that is good, you know everything about us, both good and bad, and you love us anyway. We want to live our lives to please you, and we need your guidance to show us what you most want us to do. Give us strength to resist temptation and make better choices. Forgive us for our past wrongdoings and make us right with you in how we use our bodies, our hearts, and our souls. Thank you for all you have entrusted us with, and help us to serve you in all we do. Amen."

✂ The Great Escape (10–12 minutes)

Say: "We are going to do a brief brainstorm session. There are no wrong answers, so no one should make fun of anyone else's. Our goal is to make a complete list together. Our brainstorm question is: What are some of the reasons people choose to use alcohol, drugs, or tobacco?"

Write all of the teens' responses on a large writing surface.

Divide the group into pairs and give each pair a posterboard or a large piece of paper and markers. Then say: "With your partner, I'd like you to create a billboard that illustrates how your faith responds to one of these reasons we came up with. For example, if you choose 'Everybody's doing it,' you might draw a picture of a bridge and write above it, 'Don't jump off the bridge just because everyone else is doing so.' Remember that billboards don't contain a lot of words, so you have to get your message across in simple ways. You have five minutes."

After five minutes, ask each pair to show its billboard to the group but not to say which of the reasons it addresses. Then ask the rest of the youth to guess which reason it responds to. Finally, ask, "What kinds of problems can the abuse of alcohol, drug, or tobacco create for users and for society?"

Here and Now (10–12 minutes)

Distribute pens or pencils and copies of the Considering My Choices handout on page 55. Say: "God has given us our bodies to take care of and use for good purposes. We are meant to be in relationship with God and with one another. But we sometimes make choices that are dangerous to our physical and emotional health. Ask yourself: 'Is it OK to do anything I feel like doing with my body? Is what I do with my body only up to me? Are others affected by my choices?' In your hands, you have a survey to help you think further about this topic."

Allow the youth a few minutes to complete the survey. Then ask:

• Were any of the questions hard to answer? Which ones?
• Did you ever agree and disagree with the same statement? Why or why not?
• How can you know what's best or what God would want for you?

Read aloud Ephesians 4:17-24 on page 29 of the student journal. Ask, "What do you think the Scripture is saying about caring for our bodies and our relationships?"

Say: "God made our amazing and wonderful bodies and minds. God wants us to respect the amazing creations we are—ourselves and others. Sexual activity is intended for married adults, who are prepared to handle their intimacy and any consequences of it. Our decisions about sex may affect our entire lifetime and that of others. Be prayerful and careful in your relationships. Let God fulfill any emptiness you may be trying to fill with sex."

Don't Mention It

---

what do you see?

Provide markers and posterboard or large sheets of paper. Optional: a markerboard or a chalkboard and chalk.

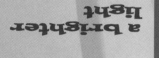

a brighter light

Provide copies of the Considering My Choices handout on page 55, pens or pencils, and a student journal.

I've Been Lied To

Think of a time when someone you cared about lied to you. Who was it? What did he or she say? Did you know right away that what the person said wasn't the truth? If not, how and when did you find out?

Write about the situation here:

_____
_____
_____
_____
_____
_____
_____

*Which phrases describe how you reacted at **first**?* (Put an F beside the words that apply.) Add any phrases that aren't listed below.

*How do you react to the situation **now**?* (Put an N beside the words that apply.) Add any phrases that aren't listed below.

I understand. ⬭
I'm sad. ⬭
I'm OK. ⬭
I'm disappointed. ⬭
I don't care. ⬭
I'm hurt. ⬭
I'm confused. ⬭
I'm angry! ⬭
I'm surprised. ⬭
I'm not surprised. ⬭

Anger Identification

Response 1: The Volcano

Explode immediately with anger

Say hurtful things or things you regret because you didn't think about them first

Realize your response was hasty or inappropriate and probably wish you hadn't said what you did

You stay angry

You don't know how to get over it without admitting you were wrong

Reconcile with or forgive the other person

You hold onto your anger

You let your anger die out

Response 2: The Shaken Soda Bottle

Anger builds and builds and bubbles up inside you

Carry it around

Decide you've ready to move on

Think about what angered you

Reconcile or move on

Carry a grudge

Feel burdened by your anger

The pressure starts to subside

Response 3: The Peacemaker

You feel angry

You acknowledge and name your emotions

You go to the source to talk through the problem

You get the problem resolved peacefully

Session 2 Reproducible Page

Scripture Search

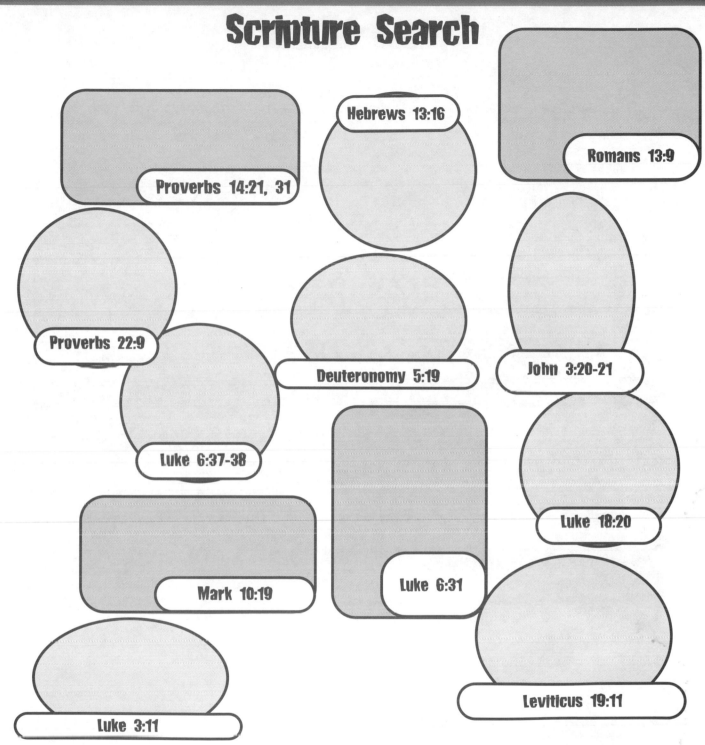

Proverbs 14:21, 31

Hebrews 13:16

Romans 13:9

Proverbs 22:9

Deuteronomy 5:19

John 3:20-21

Luke 6:37-38

Mark 10:19

Luke 6:31

Luke 18:20

Leviticus 19:11

Luke 3:11

Nothing in all creation is hidden from God's sight. Everything is uncovered and laid bare before the eyes of [God] to whom we must give account. (Hebrews 4:13 NIV)

- *How does it feel to know that God sees all we do?*

- *How would this knowledge help you to stop and think before doing something you know is not right in God's eyes?*

Session 3 Reproducible Page

Word Search

Look in all directions for words that are positive, hopeful, and faith-related.

```
A R S O F F E R T Z A H M E K I W R G H O C
R P E A C E R M I I H C A Y I S I E K X U E
T A L E Q P E A Y E I W N P N E S A J P F T
I D N F K O N R R B O O K V P W E L L P E R
S U F A I T H V T B S M I L E Y J T Y R T A
T R U S T G O S R E R T H E L A S W E R A M
I D N H A L P A U B R L S O Z F R I E N D S
M E P O C R E A T E P O V E G O O D N E W S
G R A C E H G R H O D E T I H E A L T H Y R
```

My Prayer of Forgiveness

Fill in the blanks to create your own prayer.

God, you know how hard it is for us to look beyond the hurt and the _____ we sometimes experience. We easily become _____ and negative and hold onto the pain as though we should remember it.

Now we ask you to show us the ways of forgiveness and of _____. Heal our _____ and make us _____ again so that we can live as _____ of God.

Remind us to lighten up about _____ when our unrealistic expectations have led us to disappointment. Take the heaviness from our hearts and fill us with _____ and the light of life you freely give. Help us to replace sadness with _____, hate with _____, bitterness with _____, and grudges with _____.

We thank you for holding onto us even when we sometimes let go of you. Help us to come home to you. Amen.

Session 5 Reproducible Page

May I Go With You?

Statement 1: Joe and I are going to see a movie instead of going to fifth and sixth periods at school today.

Statement 2: I'm meeting Sasha after school at the gym door so that we can take a different route home from school. We don't want to get stuck having Jessica tag along again—it's so embarrassing when our friends see us with her!

Statement 3: Wow—you wouldn't believe the magazine Jake found in his older brother's room. He's gonna let me see it tonight when his parents are gone to a meeting!

Statement 4: I can't believe Dana wrote such awful things about me in that note! I hate her and I'm never gonna forgive her! She's not my friend anymore! I'm gonna call her and tell her that.

Statement 5: We're going to the mall on Saturday. Jake really wants that new CD, and he's found a way to get that security tag off it without the store clerk noticing. I really want to hear the CD, but I sure hope he doesn't get caught. He'd get grounded for sure.

-- ✂

Let There Be Thanksgiving!

In the blanks below, write a word that starts with the letter to the left. Write only words that are pleasing, positive, Christlike, or in the Ephesians Scripture your group read today.

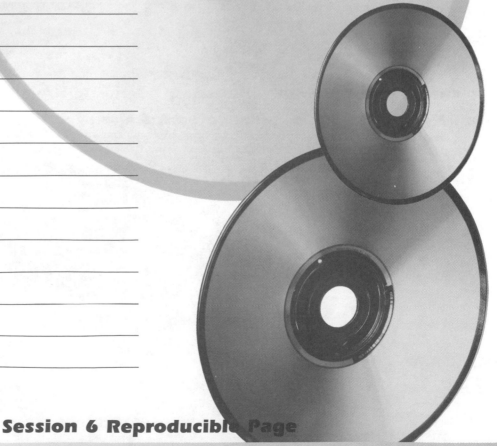

T _____
H _____
A _____
N _____
K _____
S _____
G _____
I _____
V _____
I _____
N _____
G _____

Considering My Choices

Is it OK to do anything you feel like doing to and with your body? Are these decisions up to you only? Are others affected by your choices? These are some of the things you'll consider as you work through the statements below.

Mark the Agree or Disagree column (or both) for each statement.

Statement	Agree	Disagree
I should do anything that feels good to me.	_____	_____
If I hurt my body, that action is no one's business by mine.	_____	_____
I can have sex without getting emotionally involved.	_____	_____
I don't need to be married in order to have sex.	_____	_____
My own desires come first before anyone else's.	_____	_____
I should be able to spend my money any way I want.	_____	_____
I make responsible decisions about spending my money.	_____	_____
It's OK to do something illegal as long as I don't get caught.	_____	_____
I should be able to have whatever I want, even if others go without something they need.	_____	_____
I should share what I have with others.	_____	_____
My friends try to get me to do things I don't think are good.	_____	_____
It's OK to drink because I can stop anytime I want to.	_____	_____
I should be able to do the things my parents do.	_____	_____
My friends set a good example for me most of the time.	_____	_____
My parents should let me decide what time I come home.	_____	_____
Sometimes I talk my friends into doing things they shouldn't.	_____	_____
God only sees what I do some of the time, not all of the time.	_____	_____
I can do anything I want as long as I ask for forgiveness afterwards.	_____	_____
What I do behind closed doors doesn't affect anyone else.	_____	_____
I am a good influence on my friends.	_____	_____

Session 7 Reproducible Page

Acts of Kindness

*Our kind behavior not only makes others feel good,
but it also helps us feel better about ourselves.
You may just make this day better for someone!*

Store: _____   **Date:** _____   **Your Name:** _____

Act of kindness offered to someone

_____

_____

_____

_____

_____

_____

_____

_____

_____

_____

_____

_____

_____

_____

_____

_____

_____

_____

Response from that person

_____

_____

_____

_____

_____

_____

_____

_____

_____

_____

_____

_____

_____

_____

_____

_____

_____

_____

Out and About Reproducible Page

Retreat:
"Livin' Light & Livin' Right"

Friday Evening

Introduction to the Retreat Theme

Ask the youth to close their eyes and be silent. After a few seconds, read Matthew 11:28-30 from *The Message*:

> Are you tired? Worn out? Burned out on religion? Come to me. Get away with me and you'll recover your life. I'll show you how to take a real rest. Walk with me and work with me—watch how I do it. Learn the unforced rhythms of grace. I won't lay anything heavy or ill-fitting on you. Keep company with me and you'll learn to live freely and lightly.

Provide table games and flashlights or candles if there is no campfire site at your retreat location.

Invite everyone to follow you or a designated youth in silence to a campfire or dark space outdoors where you can use flashlights or candles. Along the way, pause in a dark spot, with no lights on. Ask:

- What are some good things about the dark?

- What things are not so good about the dark?

Continue toward the gathering spot. Say: "Dwight Moody said that 'character is what a person is in the dark.' A similar quotation from Russell W. Gough is, 'Character is what you do when no one is watching.' "

Ask:

- Do you feel that darkness gives you freedom or tempts you to do things you might not do in places where someone could see you? If so, how?

- What are some things people do in the dark when they think no one can see them?

- Do you ever have thoughts at night that bring on feelings of sadness, loneliness, or even fear?

When your group arrives at the gathering spot, say: "I guess it could be both bad news and good news that God can see us clearly whether it's dark or light, whether we talk to God or ignore God, whether we make wise choices or poor choices. God remains with us always, and God's light will show us the way if we only pay attention."

Retreat: "Livin' Light and Livin' Right"

Ask the youth to light their candles or turn on their flashlights if a campfire is not already going. Sing a quiet song or two.

Close by saying: "We are meant to live as children of the light, where God sees everything. How should we live so that what is exposed is good, as God intends? By letting God lead the way."

If you have a campfire, enjoy some informal time around the fire. If not, go back to your other meeting area and play table games.

Nighttime Preparations

Give the youth free time until 11:15, then ask them to get ready for bed. Turn out the lights by 11:45, and allow 15 minutes for talking in the dark.

Saturday

Time with God

Hand out the student journals and and give the youth time to complete the pages in silence. If the youth have already completed their journals, ask them to take a quiet walk, read the Bible, meditate and pray, or write in their personal journals.

Step Together

Gather the group and assign one youth the role of Reader. With the rest of the group, form either one circle or several small circles, depending on the size of your group. Ask the youth to stand shoulder-to-shoulder. Say: "You'll be given instructions to step back or forward. Do not move if the instruction doesn't apply to you." Then ask the Reader to give the following instructions, pausing after each one so that the group members can follow it:

Step back if you have ever told a lie.
Step back if you have ever not told the whole truth.
Step back if you have been lied to.
Step back if you have ever hurt someone's feelings.
Step back if someone has hurt your feelings.
Step back if you have ever called someone a name or put someone down.
Step back if you have been called names or been put down.
Step back if you have ever cheated on a test or in a game.
Step back if you have played a game in which another person was cheating.
Step back if someone has ever copied or tried to copy your answers.
Step back if you have used swear words.
Step back if you have ever talked too much without saying anything.

Provide table games if there is no campfire.

10:45	Free Time
11:15	Prepare for Bed
11:45	Lights Out!

Saturday

8:00	Breakfast
9:00	Time With God

Provide student journals.

9:30	Step Together

If possible, conduct this activity outside or in a large room.

Flip the Switch: Living in the Christ Light

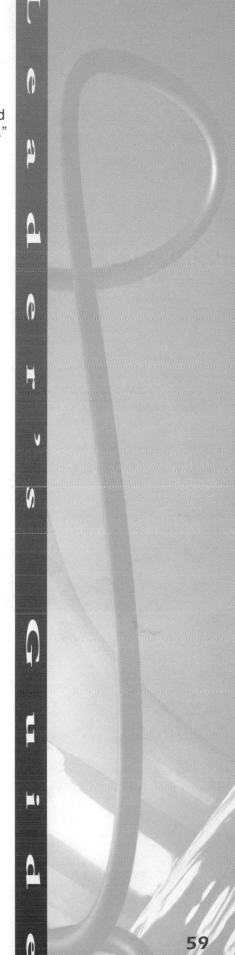

Step back if you ever had enough but wanted more.
Step back if you have ever treated your body with disrespect.
Step back if someone else has ever treated your body with disrespect.
Step back if you have ever held a grudge against someone else.
Step back if you are still holding a grudge against someone else.

Ask: "How does it feel to be separated by harmful things that others do to us and that we do to others? Do you want to keep living this way, or would you rather mend the damage if possible?" Say, "Here's a chance to do so." Ask the Reader to give the following instructions:

Step forward if you usually tell the truth.
Step forward if you have told someone you are sorry for what you did to them.
Step forward if you have ever asked for forgiveness.
Step forward if you have resisted the temptation to cheat on a test or in a game.
Step forward if you have worked to obtain something for someone who needed it.
Step forward if you have tried to stop swearing and want to use better language.
Step forward if you have been kind to someone you didn't know.
Step forward if you have said nice things to build someone up.
Step forward if you have been truly happy for someone else who got something he or she needed, earned, or wanted.
Step forward if you have resisted the temptation to do something you wanted to do but knew was wrong.
Step forward if you have tried to help a friend resist doing something harmful.
Step forward if you have worked to resolve a conflict rather than letting it get worse.
Step forward if you have resisted the temptation to buy something you couldn't afford or didn't need.
Step forward if you have helped others feel as though they belong.
Step forward if you have given God the credit for the good things in your life.
Step forward if you pray for others in need.
Step forward if you ask God to help you know God's will for your life.

Ask, "How does it feel to know that your choices brought you either closer to or further away from God and others?"

Say: "God lets us choose. Separating ourselves from one another and, consequently, from God is a choice that is demonstrated by our behavior. If you want to grow closer to God, try doing some of the 'step forward' instructions."

Retreat: "Livin' Light and Livin' Right"

Schedule

10:00 Fingerpainting

Provide fingerpaint, paper, newspaper, rags or paper towels, and a sink or bucket of water for cleanup.

Before conducting this activity, spread out newspaper where the youth will complete their paintings.

11:00 Play Time

If you choose to have play time indoors, provide card or table games.

12:00 Lunch

1:30 Journals

Provide student journals.

2:00 Get Moving!

3:00 Small Groups

4:30 Free Time

Fingerpainting

Hand out the paper and fingerpaints. Invite everyone to paint a picture that represents how close he or she feels to the light or to the dark.

After the youth have finished, say: "Just like darkness can only be overcome by light, hate is only overcome by love." Then ask the youth to put the pictures in a safe place to dry, and to clean themselves up. Later put the paintings up for everyone to see.

Play Time

Give the youth free time until 11:00; then provide various card or table games. Or, if the weather and space allow, play group games outside.

Journals

Hand out the student journals again. Ask the youth to complete any pages they haven't finished, or, if they have finished, to review the pages. Tell the youth they may also use the Notes pages in the back of the journal to reflect on what they have learned during the retreat and how this knowledge can help them to live in the light.

Get Moving!

Do something physically active (such as an outdoor game, singing, or dancing) to wake everyone up.

Small Groups

Divide the group into small teams and spread the teams out around the room. Post these instructions where each group can see them:

Read these quotations and discuss what they mean to you:

"Treat everyone with politeness, even those who are rude to you, not because they are nice, but because you are" (Anonymous).

"Worry weighs a person down; an encouraging word cheers a person up" (Proverbs 12:25, NLT).

Discuss: How hard is it to treat people nicely when they aren't nice to you?

Tell your group a story of when you managed to be nice to those who weren't nice to you. When each person finishes his or her story, the rest of the group should say, "Congratulations, [name]."

Flip the Switch: Living in the Christ Light

An Act of Kindness

Hand out the supplies. Ask the youth to fold their pieces of paper in half and to make cards for people who need encouragement or just a kind word. The youth may use a church directory or another list to find names of such people.

Ask the youth to address the envelopes and prepare them for mailing. Make sure that the cards are sent as soon as possible.

Singing

Let the youth pick several of their favorite songs and sing them.

Affirmations

Divide the group into teams and have each team form a circle. Say: "Take turns having one person stand in the center. Each person in the circle should say a kind word or comment about the person in the center. All of the statements must be positive and respectful so that the person feels good about what he or she hears. The statements can be as simple as 'I like your smile.' "

Make sure each person has a chance to stand in the center of the circle. Then ask the youth to tell the whole group how it felt to be the person in the middle of the circle, discussing what they liked and didn't like.

Distribute glow sticks or ask the youth to get their flashlights. Lead the group outside toward a dark space and ask them to sit quietly. Ask the youth to reflect on the positive things people said about them. Then ask them to think about how much nicer life would be if they heard nice things about themselves every day.

One at a time, invite each person to say something he or she is thankful for then to snap the glow stick or turn on the flashlight and point it straight up. When the whole group is aglow, say this prayer:

"God of Light, you brighten our days and even our nights. You bring us happiness, peace, patience, goodness, and kindness even when we haven't earned them, all because you love us unconditionally. Help us to also love unconditionally and to treat others with kindness every chance we get. Thank you for lifting our shadows of darkness and showering us with the light of life. Amen."

Retreat: "Livin' Light and Livin' Right"

5:30   Dinner

7:00   **An Act of Kindness**

Provide 8-1/2 x 11 construction paper, business-size envelopes, stamps, pens, scissors, and glue sticks or double-sided tape. Optional: church directory.

Cut each sheet of construction paper in half. If you need additional names for this activity, you may want to contact an agency.

8:30   **Singing**

Optional: provide songbooks.

9:00   **Affirmations**
Provide glow sticks or flashlights.

10:00   **Snacks and Board Games**

11:00   **Get Ready for Bed**

11:30   **Lights Out!**

Sunday

8:00   **Breakfast**

9:00   **Pack Up and Clean Up**

9:30   **Closing Worship**
(see pages 62–63)

10:30   **Head for Home**

Worship Service: Making a Trade

Songs

Scripture

Message: Trading Darkness for Light

This worship service focuses on making choices that trade wrong for right, too much for just enough, unpleasant for pleasing, foolish talk for thanksgiving.

Sing "I am the Light of the World" and "Here I Am, Lord," or select two songs according to what the youth know and like.

Invite one of the youth to read the following Scriptures:

- "For once you were darkness, but now in the Lord you are light. Live as children of light—for the fruit of the light is found in all that is good and right and true. Try to find out what is pleasing to the Lord. Take no part in the unfruitful works of darkness, but instead expose them. For it is shameful even to mention what such people do secretly" (Ephesians 5:8-12).

- "I do not understand my own actions. For I do not do what I want, but I do the very thing I hate" (Romans 7:15).

- "Your eye is the lamp of your body. If your eye is healthy, your whole body is full of light; but if it is not healthy, your body is full of darkness. Therefore consider whether the light in you is not darkness. If then your whole body is full of light, with no part of it in darkness, it will be as full of light as when a lamp gives you light with its rays" (Luke 11:34-36).

Feel free to include your own stories in the script below to illustrate the message of trading darkness for light.

"One of the greatest things about God is that God always wants good for us. I don't know anyone else who can make that incredible guarantee. God loves us far beyond our comprehension. What greater gift could we ever want than that!

"Think about what God has helped you trade. Perhaps it's foolish talk for thanksgiving, destructive behaviors for healthier options, laziness for motivation, guilt for freedom, or tiredness for rest. Have you made any of these trades? Can you think of others? Turn to your neighbor and tell him or her two things you've gotten rid of and what you've gained instead as you've grown in your relationship with God."

Allow two minutes for discussion, then ask, "What are some of the things you traded?"

Flip the Switch: Living in the Christ Light

Say: "You can make a trade any day of your life, because God's power and love for us never end. Think of something you would like to get rid of and something you would like to receive instead. When you have thought of something, raise your hand, and when I call on you say, 'I want to make a trade!' Then tell us what you're trading." Wait for responses. If the youth have trouble thinking of trades, remind them of the ones you described earlier. The youth may choose one of those trades or a trade someone else mentions if it applies to them.

Hand out pens and student journals or index cards. Say: "You now have an opportunity to write your own oath. An oath is a promise, with God as your witness." If the youth have their student journals, ask the youth to turn to page 32. Say, "Write out the following sentence and fill in the blanks with your own choice of words: *From this time on I am going to try my best to trade away [blank] and replace it with [blank].*"

When everyone is finished writing, ask one of the youth to say, "Please join me in prayer" and to read aloud the following prayer:

"God of all that is good and right in our lives, you have heard our oaths to make a change for the better. We ask your help in knowing how to achieve these goals. Thank you for lightening our load and lighting our pathway so that we can live light and live right! Amen."

Have another youth deliver the following benediction:

"May you go from here a renewed person whose thoughts express faith, whose words express wisdom, whose deeds express kindness, and whose life expresses service. Go in peace. Amen."

Provide pens and student journals or index cards.

Prayer

Benediction

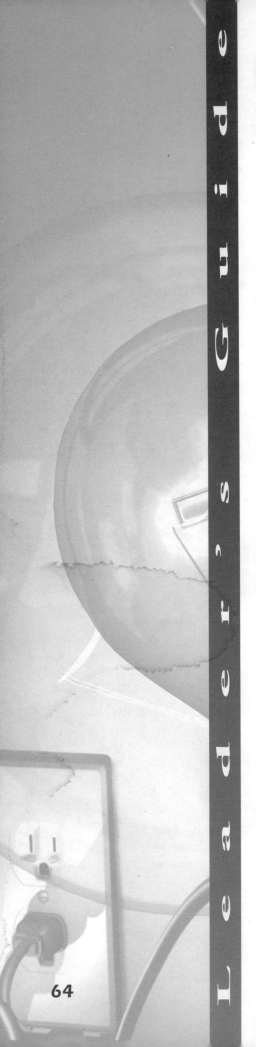

Out and About: Acts of Kindness

Purpose of This Outing

In this outing, youth may practice and evaluate how kindness affects them and those around them.

Preparation

Prior to the outing, gather pens and make copies of the Acts of Kindness handout on page 56.

This outing can be done in a few hours. Select a busy grocery store or other variety store as the location, schedule the outing for when the store is busy, and arrange transportation for your group.

Outing Time

Before you leave, say to the youth: "We have all heard the phrase *random acts of kindness*. Today we are going to practice these acts by going to a busy store. Our goal is to walk through the store as though we were shopping, stopping to look at things and acting naturally. If we act suspiciously, this activity won't work.

"As you walk around, watch for opportunities to be kind to people. The things you can most likely do are to step aside to let someone with a cart by, and to reach for something that a person can't easily reach. Or you could lift something heavy for a person who has difficulty lifting. Your acts of kindness don't have to be big, however. One of the nicest things you can do may be something as small as smiling at someone.

"We will walk around in pairs for your comfort and safety. You may need to take turns helping people, since others probably won't need the help of two people in this setting. Be aware of your surroundings and observe people without staring at them. You will log your experiences on the Acts of Kindness handout." Tell the youth when and where to regroup.

After the walk through the store, gather the youth and distribute pens and copies of the Acts of Kindness handout on page 56. Ask the youth to write down their acts of kindness and the responses they got. Then ask them to discuss what they wrote.

Another Option

If you have time, conduct this activity at a different location such as a mall. Ask the youth to smile at people they pass and to notice the shoppers' responses.